ALL OF YOU

Alex Benkast

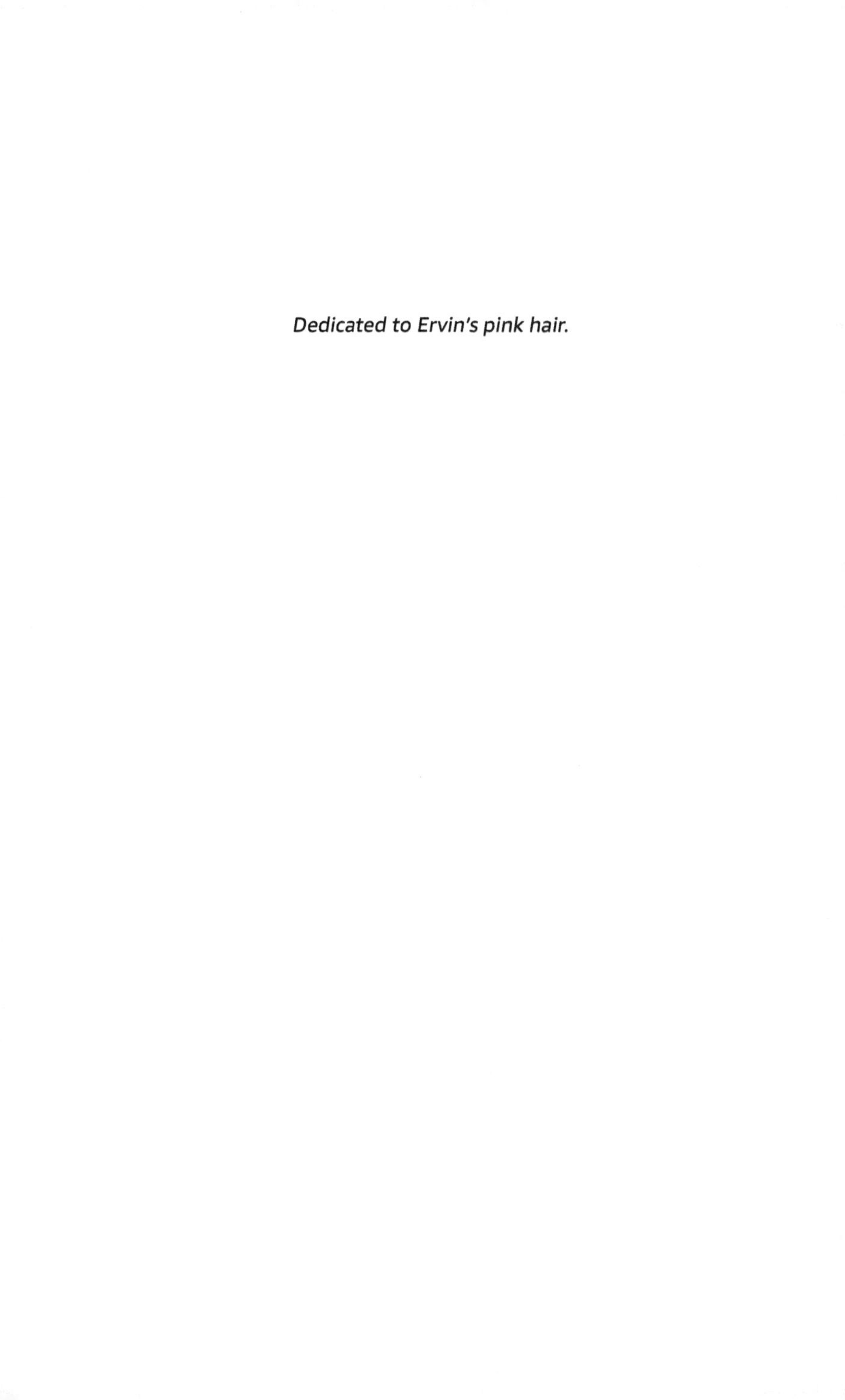

Dedicated to Ervin's pink hair.

CHAPTER 1

Charming intruders &
questionable self-portraits

"Why would anyone want a 13-foot self-portrait in their home?"

The question came from Juan's best friend Noelia, who was lounging on the couch, gesturing at the soon-to-be-painted wall.

Juan swept a hand over his buzzed hair. The answer was simple. "Because I can." He'd built his multimillion-dollar empire through relentless hard work and determination. To him, the painting represented his family's journey out of poverty.

"How much are you paying that obscure artist?"

"800k."

"*Dollars*, not pesos?" Noelia coughed. "Sure they're legit?"

Juan plopped down next to his sister, who, despite being only thirteen months older, was arguably wiser. The artwork would depict his naked back, not his face, because a 13-foot portrait of his face staring back at him would give him the creeps too.

Juan wasn't familiar with the painter, Lin Solavida, a local world-class artist specializing in hyper-realistic paintings, but they came highly recommended by one of his famous musician friends. "If they're good enough for Marc, they're good enough for me."

Noelia's eyes sparkled as she leaned forward. "So, you're going to play 'catching Santa?'"

That was the strange part. No one had ever laid eyes on Lin Solavida, and to add to the mystery, the artist had requested that Juan stay out of the room throughout the several-week painting process.

"I'm tempted," Juan admitted. Lin Solavida was obviously a fabricated name. It gave off a feminine vibe to him, yet the word around town was that Lin was a middle-aged man with a Quasimodo-like hunchback.

"When's the painter going to start this questionable masterpiece?"

Juan glanced at the gleaming Rolex on his wrist. "In about fifteen minutes, so we better 'vacate the premises' as per the contract," he said, gesturing with air quotes.

He rose from his seat and extended a hand to help Noelia up from the couch.

"They better make you resemble that *Avengers* guy," she said. "Just, you know, more Captain Colombia."

"Shut up," he chuckled, giving her ear a gentle flick.

You knew you had made it when Hollywood came knocking on your door. Even though it was a minor role that further solidified his panty-dropper image, the family movie Juan had chosen for his acting debut would be streamed worldwide.

The incredible soundtrack alone was worth it. He foresaw the songs being replayed endlessly, much like composer Lin-Miguel Santos' other catchy, award-winning hits throughout the years. Just imagining the cascade of both admiration and curses from tired parents made Juan smile.

His plan was to pop open a bottle of champagne the moment he spotted his artist name, Manolo, in the rolling credits. It would be hands down the most satisfying response to all his doubters.

"Of course, I'll be there for the premiere," Juan assured his agent over the phone as he rounded the corner into the entrance hall, preparing for his morning run. He would subject himself to rigorous Covid testing just to walk the red carpet alongside the likes of Lin-Miguel Santos, and his mother's favorite Colombian-American actor, John Torrado.

Nothing could stop him.

Except—

Shit, the wall.

No, not the wall.

Juan winced, rubbing his side where it smarted from the collision. He glanced down at the person he'd knocked to the ground.

There was a woman in his house! And not his ancient, toothless housekeeper. This was a young woman with dark brown hair tied up in a mustard-colored headscarf. She sported rolled-up ripped jeans, white sneakers, and a black tank top that accentuated every beautiful curve.

Her full lips formed a surprised "O."

Should he call the police on the intruder, or extend her a helping hand? Manners or self-preservation? That was the question.

"Are you armed?" he blurted, his mind racing.

Laughing, she shook her head.

It wasn't a chilling, "I'll lock you up in my basement" laugh, but rather a charming, "What just happened?" kind of laugh.

Juan reached out his hand and helped her up. She smelled of acrylic paint and Sexy Intrigue, an intoxicating blend of floral and vanilla scents.

"Angelina," she said, biting her lip to stifle her smile. "But you can call me Lina."

"Juan. Nice to meet you. What are you doing in my house?"

She gave him a once-over, taking in his crisp white sneakers, black athletic shorts, and a T-shirt divided into equal color blocks of beige, black, and white. Something about it made a dimple on Lina's cheek wink at him.

The tip of her tongue darted out and she swiped it across her lip as she studied his face.

Juan cleared his throat, trying to break the growing tension. Then he gave her a look he hoped conveyed, "So? Why are you invading my space?"

Lina blinked, then motioned with her thumb toward the hallway behind her. "I can't believe I'm saying this, but I'm working here."

"Lina... as in Lin Solavida, the artist who's painting my big-ass mural?"

She bit her lip again and nodded. "At least you're aware that this is probably the biggest Ode to Self the world's ever seen."

He grasped the back of his neck. "Yeah, well, it's a metaphorical middle finger to all the people who doubted me."

"Must've been a lot of people, judging by the size of that thing," she muttered under her breath.

"You have no idea," he muttered back. Then he gestured toward the hallway. "How's it going?" She'd been working on the painting for over a week now. Was it too much to hope she was almost done so he could reclaim his third-favorite room?

Lina clutched her elbow, hesitating for a moment before striding down the hallway, calling back to him, "Are you coming or what?"

Shaking his head, Juan followed her into the living room and came to a halt in front of the wall.

A work platform stood about a foot high in front of it. The upper portion of the wall was covered in a rough outline, while the lower part depicted his jeans-clad butt and bare lower back.

"Nice ass, by the way," Lina remarked. She was working from a real picture, and that was his real ass.

"I work out."

"I can tell. Looks like that's all you do."

Juan stroked his beard. "Funny, you make it sound like an insult. Usually, women appreciate the ripped, 'I can bench press a baby elephant' look."

"Under normal circumstances, I might dig it too. But I have to spend twelve hours a day staring at this —" Lina tapped the poster-sized photograph of his naked, tattooed body. "I'm sweating and horny, and questioning my life choices."

After letting out an exaggerated sigh, she said, "Maybe I should just refund your money and call it a day."

"Oh no, no, no. You have to finish this," he insisted, stepping forward and placing his hands on Lina's shoulders.

She tilted her head back and groaned, a strangely sexy sound.

"What do you need?" he asked, willing to offer her pretty much anything. When he set his mind to something, he followed through. And that meant she had to follow through too.

"I don't know. A bottle of *aguardiente* and an orgasm?" she said with a shrug.

"Okay," he rubbed his hands together, "I can do that."

Lina slapped her hands to her face. "Man, I was joking."

"About what?"

"The day-drinking, and more importantly, the idea of accosting a stranger. Go! I'll be fine." She shooed him out of the room.

Lin Solavida, Ladies and Gentlemen. Quasimodo my ass!

***

Outside, Juan slipped on his earbuds and speed-dialed his sister.

"I caught Santa," he exclaimed. "I repeat: I caught Santa."

Noelia's excited squeal resonated through the phone. "Tell me everything."

"*He* is a smoking hot *Mrs*. Claus!" Juan revealed.

"No way!"

"She's cute and funny, and she kicked me out of my own damn house."

"Aww."

As Juan began his warm-up stretches, he stole a glance at the glass walls of his two-story mansion. Although he couldn't see her, he knew she had a view of him.

"There's a beautiful woman in my house," he emphasized his current dilemma. After spending the past two years of the global pandemic single and isolated within the confines of his home, Lina's presence was a welcome change.

"Then try to get to know her," his sister suggested.

"How?" He wasn't allowed into the room. Lina's unwavering stance just minutes ago was a clear indication she wouldn't budge on that request.

"Since you can't go to her, make her come to you. Turn up the heat—figuratively and literally."

The room Lina was working in had a climate control feature. Two floor-to-ceiling window panels offering a stunning view of his backyard and pool occupied the space on either side of the wall she was painting.

An idea sparked in Juan's mind. He could work out in front of those windows. He could also do it with a distracting amount of noise.

***

After working up a sweat, Juan headed to the outdoor shower, refreshing himself before cooling off in his infinity pool. From the poolside, he gazed out at the breathtaking vista of lush green hills that stretched beyond his Bucaramanga estate.

He swam a few invigorating laps before he reclined on one of the chaise lounges positioned in the shallow end of the pool near the glass windows.

With his phone in hand, he glanced over his shoulder. Through the glass, he caught sight of Lina standing on the work platform, her paintbrush delicately poised against the wall. Despite her apparent stillness, Juan recognized the mastery of her hyperrealistic technique, knowing every stroke she made would capture even the finest details, including his pores. He could hardly wait to see the finished mural.

The rush of excitement stayed with him as he initiated the first part of his plan.

He opened the Smart Home app on his phone and cranked up the thermostat in the living room to a higher temperature than ever before. Bucaramanga was warm year-round, so he'd never tested the AC system's full capacity.

As he relaxed in his chair, he leaned back and listened to music, eagerly anticipating Lina's reaction as the temperature climbed.

Thirty minutes passed, yet there was no sign of the painter. Juan couldn't resist peeking through the window once more. To his surprise, Lina remained on the work platform, but she had removed her tank top, revealing a black lace bralette that hugged her breasts. He couldn't help but appreciate her beauty. A generous handful, he imagined, flexing his hand.

Amused by Lina's unwavering determination, Juan grabbed his phone and adjusted the temperature a few degrees higher. If he were in her position, he'd already be in an ice bath.

It took another twenty minutes before Lina finally opened the glass door, her face glistening with sweat and strands of glossy hair clinging to her temples. The red flush on her cheeks could be from the heat —or her evident anger, as her glare pierced through him with lethal intensity.

Oh shit.

CHAPTER 2

Wet jeans & an injured wrist

Without a word, Lina marched towards the edge of the pool and dived in, resurfacing with a grimace still etched on her face.

"There's something wrong with your AC. It feels like a billion degrees in there. I can't work like this."

Juan rose from the chaise lounge and strolled over to the patio door. As he stepped inside, the heat assaulted him. He couldn't help but be amazed that Lina had endured it for that long.

Thankfully, she hadn't fainted on the work platform. What a stupid idea—even if it had achieved the intended effect.

Juan ran a hand over his face. "Sorry. I'll get the AC fixed right away," he assured her, avoiding direct eye contact as he got up and walked over to the bar.

He grabbed a water bottle and a towel for Lina and placed them both on the chaise lounge beside his. Returning to his own towel, he sat down and called his sister. "Hey, can you come fix the AC?"

Noelia snorted with amusement. "You've done it, my devious brother!"

"Uh-huh, thanks," he said before ending the call and adjusting the temperature to a more comfortable level.

He returned his attention to Lina, who was struggling to remove her wet jeans. Cracking a joke wouldn't be the appropriate response in this situation, particularly with her current mood, so Juan offered cautiously, "Need some help?"

"Not humiliating at all." She spoke through clenched teeth as she settled onto the chaise. Then she picked up the water bottle and downed it in a few swift gulps.

Guilt twinged in his gut as he contemplated what to do. "We don't have to make this a big deal. I can close my eyes while I help you remove them," he suggested, hoping to ease her discomfort.

With a slight shake of her head, Lina directed her gaze towards the sky as she unbuttoned and unzipped her jeans, revealing a tantalizing glimpse of black lace panties. "Fine, set me free."

After he assisted her in removing the damp fabric, they settled into a comfortable silence. The tight sensation in his stomach eased the more Lina's features and posture began to relax.

A while later, their peaceful interlude was interrupted when the music shifted to the soundtrack of his upcoming movie. To Juan's astonishment, Lina began singing along to some of the lyrics, a familiarity that shouldn't have been possible since the music hadn't been released to the public yet.

Juan narrowed his eyes, studying her. "Do you know these songs?"

Lina returned his gaze with a quizzical look. "Maybe. Why?"

"You're not supposed to. Where did you hear them?"

Removing the black elastic from her wrist, Lina tied her hair into a bun atop her head. "I know the composer. He's my godfather," she revealed, her explanation only deepening the mystery surrounding her.

"Lin-Miguel Santos is your godfather?" Juan gave her an approving nod. "You just became way cooler."

Lina responded with a smile and an affectionate eye roll. "He's amazing."

As they both admired the golden glow of the sunset and the breathtaking landscape surrounding them, Juan couldn't contain his excitement any longer. "I'm in the movie."

"You're kidding."

Juan raised his hands in a gesture of sincerity. "I swear. It's a small role, but still, being part of such a cool project is pretty special."

In a quiet voice, Lina revealed, "My dad is in the movie too."

Juan tried to piece the puzzle together and identify who among the cast could be her father. Assuming he and Lina were similar in age, he narrowed it down to two possibilities.

"Don't tell me your dad is John Torrado," he said, though he knew it didn't make much sense given the actor was married with two children, neither of whom was named Angelina.

The tension radiating from Lina, evident in the clenching of her jaw, confirmed he'd hit the bullseye with his guess.

Interesting.

"Forget I said anything." Lina crossed her arms and directed her gaze straight ahead. "Do you think they fixed the AC?"

Deciding to table the sensitive conversation for another time, Juan rose from his seat and headed inside to check the room temperature. To his relief, it had been restored to a comfortable level.

"It's fixed," he called out to Lina.

Eager to see the progress on the mural, Juan admired her work. She'd painted up to below his shoulder blades, creating a remarkably realistic depiction that seemed almost tangible.

Lost in his admiration, Juan failed to notice Lina approach him. As he turned around, they collided once again, eliciting a curse from both of them.

In an instinctive response, Juan had reached out to prevent Lina from falling.

"Why does this keep happening?" she said, her body squirming against his, causing a confusing flurry of sensations.

Lina stilled when she realized the compromising position they were in. "I'm in my underwear."

He directed his gaze toward the ceiling, fighting

the urge to let his hand drop any lower, close enough to cup her shapely behind.

Lina took a step back and uttered a quiet oath to herself. "Let's pretend none of this ever happened."

He couldn't help but scoff at the notion. As if that ever worked in real life.

With a shrug, he said, "If that's what you want."

***

Juan went three days without seeing Lina, which led him to believe she might have quit on him. He didn't have her private number, and calling her studio felt awkward, so he found himself checking his bank account for a refund.

The following morning, after his run, Juan went for a swim and then proceeded to lift weights. He'd just received a new set of equipment at his house, all part of his failing plan to impress and seduce Lina.

Midway through his workout, a rustling noise startled him, and in his attempt to prevent dropping the weight, he twisted his wrist.

Juan cursed when the pain shot through his arm.

Moments later the patio door swung open, and Lina hurriedly approached him. "Are you okay?"

He slumped forward and cradled his injured wrist. "Hell, no."

"Let's put some ice on it." Without waiting for his response, she retreated inside and returned with a bag of frozen carrots. "Close enough," she said as she handed him the makeshift ice pack.

"Thanks."

To distract himself from the pain and embarrassment, he focused on Lina's appearance. She was dressed in high-waisted, light-wash jeans paired with a forest green T-shirt that had the word 'WILD' in white letters on the front, with the 'I' shaped like a pine tree. Her long hair was loosely tied back, cascading in gentle waves over her shoulders.

"This wasn't part of the plan," he grumbled.

"Which plan?"

"The plan where I make you fall madly in love with me."

Lina's smile was gentle as she asked, "There's a plan?"

"Yup."

"Huh. Is it working?"

"Not so much."

Lina laughed softly. "If it helps, no one has ever accomplished that goal. Not that anyone has ever tried. I usually keep to myself, if you couldn't tell."

He gazed back at her. "Yeah, but why? You seem like a normal, easygoing person to me."

"There's more than meets the eye," she replied cryptically, leaving it at that before heading back inside.

With a heavy sigh, Juan made his way around the house to the front entrance and went upstairs to find solace on his 'emperor' bed. He'd commissioned the bed to be custom-made. It was a luxurious escape that helped compensate for the challenges and drawbacks of his demanding career: the lack of privacy, the manipulation from others, the absence of a structured schedule, and the overwhelming pressure to consistently produce hit songs.

Cursing under his breath, he reached for his phone, which lit up with an incoming call from his sister. "I was just about to call you."

"You sound down. Everything okay?"

He exhaled another frustrated breath. "I nearly broke my wrist. But hey, Lina came out to take care of me."

"Isn't that what you wanted?"

"I want her to want me. But all I do is upset her, run her over, or, you know, embarrass myself in front of her."

Noelia chuckled. "That might actually work in your favor, bro."

Juan turned the bag of thawing carrots and applied it back onto his injured wrist. "How so?"

"Because you want something real. Perfection is boring."

His sister might be onto something. Normally, it came effortlessly for him to charm someone and secure a date, but being in this position had also made him wary. That was why his sister held such an important place in his life—she liked him for who he was, without any hidden motives. No claims of illegitimate children he supposedly fathered. No kissing and telling.

With Noelia, he could let his guard down, make mistakes, and still be loved unconditionally.

"So, what should I do?"

Noelia's response was simple. "Just relax and be

yourself. Don't force it."

"Damn, sis. That's not how I operate. I'm a doer."

His sister's voice held a hint of mischief. "Then go ahead and charm the pants off her."

CHAPTER 3

Damn you, Juan!

Forty-eight hours later, Juan came up with a new plan to spend more time with Lina, hopeful that this one didn't end in glares and injuries too. He still had much to discover about her, but one thing he already knew was how much she enjoyed her godfather's music.

Enter the state-of-the-art sound system that he could activate in every room of his house using his Smart Home app. With a tap of his finger, he blasted the movie soundtrack through the speakers, filling the air with the familiar tunes.

"Damn you, Juan!" he heard Lina's exasperated voice echoing from the living room. Within seconds, the agitated artist stood before him. "You scared the crap out of me. I messed up your shoulder blade because of you. How about a little warning next time?"

Brushing past her, Juan made his way into the living room to inspect the alleged disaster. He found only a minuscule black line that had deviated from the tattoo on his shoulder, visible only upon close examination.

"You're so damn talented," he marveled, his gaze locked on the mesmerizing 3D image. She should have charged him more for her extraordinary work. "Look at this, it's as if it's coming out of the wall."

Lina stood on the scaffolding beside him, examining her work with a critical eye. "This part looks a little sloppy," she remarked, pointing to the beginning of his elbow in the painting. In the depiction, he stood with his arms raised.

Juan failed to see any flaws in the area she indicated. "You're a genius," he praised her, bowing playfully.

After patting his chest, Lina turned and descended from the scaffolding. He followed her.

The infectious beat of the song playing in the room blended seamlessly with Lina's voice as she sang along. Caught up in the moment, Juan reached out, clasped her hand, and guided her into an impromptu dance.

She hesitated for about ten seconds before she let him twirl her across the living room floor. As they kept singing along, they embodied the theatrics and passion of a Broadway performance.

Eventually, they collapsed onto the sofa, overcome with laughter and breathlessness.

"That felt surprisingly amazing," Lina admitted, taking a sip from the glass on the coffee table.

Juan lowered the volume of the music and then

reached for the glass as Lina set it down, finishing the water. "You seem really connected to these songs."

"Considering they're about me and my life, I guess that makes sense." Instead of elaborating on this bombshell news, Lina got up and took the empty glass with her.

Juan followed her into the adjacent kitchen. "What did you just say?"

"You heard me." She held the glass up to the fridge and refilled it with water before taking another sip. Apparently, she didn't mind sharing his germs either.

"You have a gift," he said, gesturing towards the living room. In the movie, everyone possesses a unique power except for a young girl who must learn to embrace her own individuality. "How are these songs about you?"

"Because it's not about talent. I'm the one no one can talk about. The one no one wants around."

Leaning against the kitchen island, he faced her with his arms crossed. "What could you have possibly done that's so terrible?"

"I'm the illegitimate child. My birth mother didn't want me, and the woman my father married didn't care much for me either. So I left. It's as if I never existed, so everyone else can be happy."

"Except you," he said, pulling her into a hug.

Lina held onto him tighter than he expected. He couldn't help but feel the weight of her self-imposed invisibility—the woman created breathtaking art but denied herself the rewards she deserved.

Yes, it wasn't his place to interfere. But he recognized his own nature—he might not resist liberating her from her gilded cage, even if it meant crossing boundaries.

"You complicate everything," she whispered against his chest, her words tinged with vulnerability. "You're the first client who doesn't follow the rules."

He chuckled as he released her. "Do I strike you as someone who follows the rules? Sometimes, you *can* judge a book by its cover. You should have known better."

"Your offer was too tempting to resist," she confessed. "I've never undertaken a project of that scale or for that amount of money." A faint laugh escaped her. "Look at me, I'm a self-made millionaire."

"You deserve to be among those ranks." His hands found her hips, igniting a magnetic pull between them.

Lina tilted her head back, their lips teasingly close, her warm breath caressing his skin. The desire to bridge the remaining gap, to embrace and kiss her fully, surged within him. Yet, a voice of reason reminded him of her vulnerability. His mother and sister would disapprove if he took advantage of her current state.

So he took a deep breath and turned to the side, breaking their intense connection.

Lina mirrored his action. "I should get back to

work so you can have your living room back in this millennium."

As Lina left the room, Juan grabbed a glass of water and settled down to observe her artistic process. Thankfully, she allowed him to witness her paint his tattoo with the same skill as his tattoo artist. He contemplated commissioning her for his next design as he appreciated the dedication and passion she poured into her craft.

An hour passed, and Lina remained engrossed in the painting, her gaze unwavering.

Juan left the room and ordered dinner, a variety of comforting Colombian dishes: *arepas*, *platanos*, *ajiaco*, beans and rice, yuca bread…

When the food arrived forty minutes later, Lina was still working on his shoulder tattoo, making minimal progress due to its intricate nature.

The smell of the food on his coffee table finally caught her attention. "You're not at the movies, Juan. You can't just eat and watch me work."

He smirked and motioned toward the table filled with local delicacies. "Do you really think I can eat all that food by myself?"

She shrugged. "You work out a lot, so your energy must come from somewhere."

This time *he* rolled his eyes at her. "Bring your fine ass down here, Lina. The food's getting cold."

Lina straightened her posture, taking her time to clean her brush before settling on the couch beside him.

Her stomach growled.

Juan tilted his head. "If you're so hungry, why didn't you take a break and eat something?"

"Because I get so immersed in my work that I forget," she said, reaching for an *arepa*.

That was the downside of being in a flow state—he too forgot to eat when he was immersed in his music.

Normally, Juan would have attempted to pull her into a conversation, but Lina remained focused on her meal, so they sat in silence.

When she slowed down, he said, "I'm going to see your dad at the premiere a week from today. Want me to give him a message?"

She paused chewing for a moment, then continued for a few more seconds before replying, "No need. I doubt he remembers me."

"Come on, Lina. There's no way he forgot you're his kid. It couldn't have been that long since you left. You're what, in your early twenties?"

"Twenty-five. I left ten years ago."

It was longer than he'd expected, but not enough time to forget she existed.

"Don't say anything to him, okay?"

"I can't make that promise. I think it's a shitty thing he did, letting you go."

"I chose to leave."

"So he was a good dad then?"

"Yes," she said without hesitation.

"But he chose his new family over you," he stated what he believed to be the underlying issue.

"Yes." Her eyes shimmered, but instead of letting

her tears fall, she stuffed her mouth with a yuca roll.

Despite her remarkable strength and independence, it made him sad that she felt she had to face life alone. "When I hurt my wrist you didn't hesitate to help me. Why don't you want me to return the favor?"

"Because," she said with enough force that he braced himself for a tough argument, only to be surprised when she couldn't even provide a lame reason. She didn't even finish her sentence. Then she wagged her finger at him. "I see what you're doing. But can we just accept that I don't want someone to hold my hand?"

He didn't believe her, so he took her hand, only to be surprised again when she didn't resist. "I don't know what kind of men you're used to, but this half-assed attempt at pushing me away isn't going to work."

She groaned, but instead of letting go of his hand, she used her free hand to gesture. "Why are you so dead-set on helping me?"

"Because I like you, and I think you could use someone to have your back for a change. You didn't deserve to be abandoned. You were just a child. The adults in your life made some seriously stupid choices."

This time, she let go of his hand and propped her elbows on her knees, dropping her head. "I think your plan is working," she grumbled.

"My plan?" It took him a moment to catch the meaning of what she was saying. "Oh, *that* plan." He grinned. "It's actually working?"

She narrowed her eyes at him. "Aren't you proud of yourself."

Her reaction only served to make his grin grow wider.

Juan smoothed his hands over his chest, and she smacked his shoulder.

"Stop that."

He puffed out his chest, snatched his phone from the couch cushion next to him, and played LMFAO's "Sexy And I Know It."

Then he got up and danced while Lina sat there shaking her head, trying to hide her smile.

She let him continue for a few seconds before she paused the song on his phone. "Are you ever going to kiss me?"

He eyed her for a moment before he continued dancing. "Yeah, but not like this."

"And what's 'this?'"

He sat back down. "Emotional, but for the wrong reasons. You're hurting, Lina. I want to kiss you when you're so turned on you can't think straight."

She nodded. "I respect that."

He pulled her into his arms. "You're truly something special."

Lina nuzzled his neck. "So are you. I can't believe this is my life right now."

CHAPTER 4

You seem like trouble to me

When Lina woke up the following morning, her body was drenched in sweat and her breathing labored. To make it even more frustrating, the throbbing sensation between her legs left no doubt about the intensity of her desire.

"Damn you, Juan, you sexy dream invader," she uttered to herself, acknowledging that for the longest time, she had no one else to confide in but herself.

Of all the men who could have slipped past her armor, Juan Fernando Peláez Gaitana was the most dangerous option, not because of his bad boy looks, but because of his fame and the exclusive, judgmental world he represented—a world she no longer belonged to.

And then there were the reservations she had about Manolo, Juan's "Macho Latino" persona. Despite his ability to create beautiful love songs, the provocative hits he occasionally produced garnered significant criticism. Still, she could admit that their time together had revealed a depth to him that went beyond the surface image.

"What am I doing here?" Lina questioned herself in front of the mirror before stepping into the shower. Whatever was happening between her and Juan was doomed to fail anyway. So why get involved with a guy who would inevitably leave her because of an irreparable flaw she believed she carried since birth?

The walls she had built around her were there for a reason.

"Just stick with the plan," she reminded herself as she got dressed: black canvas shoes paired with ripped, high-waisted black jeans, and a rust-colored knitted crop top that accentuated the yellow undertones in her light brown skin.

She gathered her hair into a stylish bun on top of her head. To complete her outfit, she picked out long golden chain earrings adorned with tiny tassels near the earlobe in shades of red, orange, and pink.

Then, on her tiptoes, she applied her minimal makeup: a touch of a dark eyebrow pencil, a swipe of lip gloss, and a fine dusting of orangey-brown eyeshadow. She appreciated her naturally long and full eyelashes because they spared her the hassle of removing mascara each night.

On her way to her car a few minutes later, she passed the full-length mirror in the hallway and smiled at her reflection. She couldn't deny how much fun she had experimenting with her outfits. Even more so because Juan looked at her with obvious admiration for her style.

Conversely, she had concluded that Juan looked his best *without* clothes, confidently displaying his chiseled abs and pecs. His well-sculpted body was a masterpiece, and she couldn't blame him for wanting to showcase his hard work.

Her smile broadened as she hopped into her car. She'd wager half her commission that Juan would find a way to flaunt his muscles when she saw him later.

***

When Lina arrived at Juan's mansion later that morning, she was taken by surprise. As she let herself in, a cute Australian Shepherd puppy greeted her with enthusiastic circles and a wagging tail. She scooped up the little fur baby, who tried to lick her chin.

Juan, dressed *only* in sweatpants the color of watermelon, entered the foyer, his gaze lingering on her from head to toe.

"Lina."

"Juan."

With a seductive smile, he approached her.

"Who's your little friend?" she asked, handing him the excited puppy.

"Angelina, whose full name I have yet to discover, meet Ervin Peláez Gaitana, the newest addition to my family."

She stroked the dog's back. "Pleasure to meet you, Ervin. I'm Angelina Isabel Torrado Valencia but I go by Lina."

"Man, I still think it's so cool that John Torrado is your dad."

Something in her chest twinged every time she heard her father's name. All her favorite childhood memories involved him. It was the two of them against the rest of the world for the first eight years of her life.

They hadn't had much: a small studio apartment in a less desirable neighborhood, a worn-out Toyota with a mind of its own, and a pocketful of dreams that eventually became a reality. Her father had a genuine love for acting and excelled at it. During her childhood, she spent countless hours in theaters, sketching the actors on stage with unwavering dedication. Even at a young age, her talent was undeniable, and her father worked extra hard to ensure she pursued her passion as well.

Lina swallowed the lump in her throat before speaking, "I need to get going. I'm a little behind schedule." She knew getting his tattoos right was a challenge, as they were intricate designs crafted by a skilled artist.

Juan's smile faded. She couldn't be sure if it was due to the delay or her sudden withdrawal, but Lina didn't stick around to find out. Instead, she proceeded to the living room, unpacking and arranging her tools precisely as she preferred.

Then she picked up the photo of Juan from the floor and studied it once more, committing every detail of his back to memory. A smile tugged at her lips as she realized she was likely the only one who was that familiar with his every mole, scar, and contour.

Despite the distracting allure his image held, she had to admit she loved capturing him in her painting.

"You like what you see?" Juan's voice broke her concentration, making her startle and nearly drop the picture.

"*Hijueputa*," she cursed, her hand clutching her racing heart.

"You were smiling," he said, pointing at the photograph.

And still no shirt on the man.

"You know why I'm falling behind with this painting?" She prodded his taut abs with her finger. "*You*. You keep distracting me."

He hooked his fingers under the waistband of her jeans and pulled her closer to him. "You know what makes life more fun?" His hand slid over her hip and paused on her butt. "*Allowing* yourself time to have fun."

She didn't know whether it was residual horniness or continued frustration, but she pushed up against him and pressed her lips to his with enough heat and hunger to revive her libido. It was liberating to have what she so desperately wanted.

Within moments, Juan had her turned around, sandwiched between him and the wall.

His breath tickled her neck as he said, "Damn, that was one frenzied kiss," before nibbling on her earlobe.

She panted when his growing erection pressed against her butt. Heat pooled between her thighs as the heel of his palm connected with where she was needy and throbbing.

Lina bucked her hips, hoping for the friction she craved, but Juan removed his hand and stepped away.

At least his chest was heaving too.

"Why'd you stop?" she asked, catching her breath. "I'm turned on if you couldn't tell."

Propping one hand on his hip, he swiped the other over the stubble on his jaw. "Oh, I could tell."

"Then what is it this time?"

"I'm not just going to take you against the wall and call it a day. If I wanted a fling, I'd have one."

He probably had his pick of women, given how they threw themselves at him. Apparently, she was one of them.

"I appreciate a woman who knows what she wants, but if you always need to be in control, then I'm not your guy."

She crossed her arms. "So, you want me to submit to you?"

"You are in control of *every* aspect of your life. Why not let this be the one area where you allow someone else to take care of you?"

Lina ran a hand over her face as she fessed up to her dilemma. "Even if I wanted to try that with you, I don't know if I can. Being in control has become ingrained in my brain over the past two decades."

"That's why I said 'practice.' I'm not expecting you to change overnight." He reached for her. "Come here."

She all but leaped into his arms, unable to resist the pull between them. His warmth enveloped her, giving her hope she didn't think she should feel.

Juan kissed her slowly, thoroughly, sending a tender sensation through her stomach. She wished she could hold onto that feeling.

"Wow," she whispered when he let go of her.

He smiled. "Not bad."

"Not bad?" Lina bumped him with her arm.

"Alright, relax." He raised his hands. "I felt the butterflies too."

Her radiance must have been visible from miles away.

"I love seeing you this happy," he said with such affection she had to suppress the sudden onset of tears.

Lina planted a smacking kiss on his lips, then placed her hands on his shoulders and guided him toward the door. "I need to get back to work. We can hang out later."

Noticing his raised eyebrows, she added, "If you want." Letting someone else have a say definitely wasn't something that came easy to her.

***

Spending time together later didn't end up happening. Juan had a last-minute lunch meeting, and when he texted her in the evening that she was welcome to join him upstairs once she was done, Lina was so absorbed in her work that it was already eleven at night when she checked her phone.

You still up? she texted him. *Sorry it got so late. I didn't realize what time it was.*

Five minutes passed, and he still hadn't replied. Lina debated whether to go home without saying anything, but there was a part of her that wanted to see him before she went to bed.

And so it begins, she chided herself. *You're already getting attached.*

She tiptoed up the free-standing spiral staircase, trying not to freak out that there wasn't much to hold on to, especially with the dimmed light. Everything in Juan's house was designed to be open, bright, and airy. This included the staircase, which was more sculptural than functional. Even the second-story landing was only secured by a half panel of glass instead of a sturdy wall.

The other thing standing out to her was Juan's love for art, particularly local Colombian art. She recognized many of the sculptures and paintings in his collection. It made sense to her now why he'd hired her. The pieces were bold and colorful, fitting perfectly in his predominantly white space—his own private gallery.

The master bedroom, situated behind floor-to-ceiling glass panels, had sheer white drapes partially drawn for privacy. On the oversized bed, Juan lay on his stomach, shirtless, with his arm draped over a pillow, his sweatpants riding teasingly low.

Curled up beside him was Ervin, who woke when Lina hesitated at the entrance of the room. The affectionate dog jumped off the bed and approached her, wagging his tail. Lina lifted him into her arms, nuzzled against his soft fur, and gently placed him back on the bed.

Juan remained motionless, his deep breathing proof he was fast asleep. Lina's longing to cuddle up beside him urged her to leave. She knew she could easily fall in love with him, and the realization scared her.

With a sigh, she made up her mind to stay focused on completing the mural and keep her emotions in check.

Better safe than sorry.

CHAPTER 5

Can't touch this... or can you?

Ever since their kiss, Juan couldn't help but notice that Lina was avoiding him, which was both frustrating and intriguing because this wasn't his usual experience with the opposite sex.

Initially, he didn't think much of it when Lina lost track of time or had errands to run the next day when he was swamped with promotional interviews.

The following day, however, she avoided eye contact and emitted anxious vibes when he approached her on the scaffolding. It was as if she had a "Can't Touch This" sign flashing above her head.

In an attempt to break the tension, he invited her to join him for lunch, but she claimed she wasn't hungry. Yet, fifteen minutes later, he spotted her through the window, eating a sandwich on the sofa.

Startling her by knocking on the window, he gestured to what she was doing.

With a beat of hesitation, Lina walked over to the patio and waited for a few more seconds before opening the door.

"Why are you doing this?" he asked.

"What do you mean?"

Juan stepped past her into the room. "You know what I'm asking."

Lina pointed at the wall. "I just want to finish this."

"You'll finish it either way. That's not the reason you're keeping your distance. You're scared to let me get close to you."

She took a step toward him. "Yes, because I'll get attached and you'll move on to the next one. Why should I put myself through that?"

Oh, hell.

His heart broke for her all over again. He wished he could just snap her out of this damn isolating belief that she couldn't seem to let go. "I can't foresee how our story ends, but there's a whole lot of fun, adventure, and happiness in the middle that you're going to miss out on."

Lina closed the gap between them and rested her forehead against his shoulder.

Juan put his arms around her and breathed her in. He understood where Lina was coming from and why it was hard for her to let him in. Every ounce of intimacy she was willing to give him meant even more because of that.

But he also believed people come into our lives as lessons. Relationships are mirrors, reflecting something back to us that needs to be noticed or worked through.

"We aren't that different," he said after a while.

Lina stepped back so they could see each other. "My sister is my best friend because, A, she's awesome, and B, because I'm scared to trust others. My relationship with her is the most honest and real connection I've ever had."

Lina tucked a loose strand of hair behind her ear. "So what you're saying is whatever is going on between us is some kind of cosmic trust exercise?"

He gave her a nod and held his hand out to her. She studied it for a moment before she placed hers in his.

"I'm going to make an effort to trust you," he said, giving her hand a light squeeze, "if you make an effort to trust me."

Lina took a deep breath before she agreed. "Deal."

***

Sharing a red carpet with the people he admired was one of the proudest moments of Juan's life. He wanted to soak it all up—the specialness of the moment, the pride he felt for representing his country in a positive light, the talented people surrounding him who had welcomed him into their circle. But it was his knowledge about Lina's childhood that cast a shadow over the excitement when he saw John Torrado posing with his wife and kids, both in their teens.

The daughter, who was blond and fair-skinned like her mother, was the older of the two siblings. He figured growing up with the perception of being replaced by a younger model who actually had a loving mother must have been hard for Lina.

They appeared to be a happy family, making it all the more heartbreaking to imagine young Lina standing on the sidelines, feeling like she didn't belong.

Juan wanted to say something, to make it right for her in some way. But before he could approach Lina's dad, Lin-Miguel Santos intercepted him.

They posed for pictures together as the reporters shouted questions at them. "What inspired you to write these songs?" was one of them.

Juan asked Lin-Miguel quietly, "You're going to tell them about Lina?"

The man's eyes widened and then narrowed. "How —"

One of the younger reporters picked up on their conversation and asked, "Who is Lina?"

Lin-Miguel remained frozen in place, so Juan decided to respond. "Lina was a Colombian girl who craved acceptance from her family. She ran away because she felt misunderstood and inferior."

When the reporter responded, "You said 'was.' Did she die?" Lin-Miguel's expression turned to dread.

"No, she's very much alive," Juan clarified, clapping Lin-Miguel on the shoulder. "She became a world-class painter. She's pretty damn amazing."

"She's my god-daughter," Lin-Miguel acknowledged finally.

"She's also your biggest fan." Juan's praise brought a genuine smile to Lin-Miguel's face.

The man ushered Juan to a more private area, allowing them to speak with some degree of confidentiality. Nodding in John's direction, Lin-Miguel said, "So you know about...?"

"Yes, I know he's her dad."

Curiosity filled the man's face. "How did you...?"

"I unknowingly hired her to paint a mural in my house." A smile formed as he reminisced about their unexpected encounter.

"Are you two...?"

Now it was his turn to hesitate. "We're not together... I mean, it's not that I don't want to... She's amazing." They hadn't yet had 'the conversation' about their relationship. "It's complicated," Juan admitted, recognizing the baggage they both carried.

Lin-Miguel chuckled. "That's the lamest explanation ever. So you have a crush on her, but she's putting up walls?"

Juan scratched his temple. "Sounds about right."

"As her godfather, I feel like I should give you a speech about respect and protection."

Juan ran a hand over his hair, pleading, "God, please don't."

The man chuckled again.

"I know what people think of me," Juan said, "but I'm not a player. I would never do anything to intentionally hurt her."

Lin-Miguel extended his hand, and he shook it.

"I want to talk to him." Juan jutted his chin toward John.

"Some things are better left alone."

"It's not right... she's hurting."

"It broke his heart when she left."

"It broke her heart that he let her go."

Lin-Miguel heaved out a long sigh. "What's your plan?"

"Arrange a meeting without telling them?"

"Where? Because he's not going to fly out to Colombia and I doubt she'd come to L.A."

"Miami," they said at the same time.

***

Lina felt a mix of gratitude and annoyance when she realized that Juan must have mentioned her ongoing project to others. Her studio's answering machine, which she hadn't checked in three weeks, was now filled with voicemails from potential clients. Among them were popular Colombian singers, actors, designers, and entrepreneurs.

She squealed with excitement when she discovered a message from Manuel Campos, her favorite Colombian singer. It was a tidbit that she'd purposely kept from Juan because the media portrayed the two singers as polar opposites who didn't appreciate each other's music.

Manuel was the charismatic golden boy, while Juan embodied the sexy bad boy. It surprised her that she found herself drawn to the latter. Though, to be fair, she hadn't noticed the "bad" in Juan. All he'd done so far was bring joy to her life and make her feel desired.

Life was good—so unbelievably good in fact that she wanted to ride the high vibes train for as long as she could.

So she made Manuel Campos her first callback. It took great effort not to show her giddiness, but her favorite singer turned out to be sweet and easygoing. They scheduled a lunch meeting for the next day to discuss his vision for the project.

After making a few more phone calls and gathering her art supplies, Lina drove over to Juan's place to finish painting his arms. Compared to the parts of his body that were covered in ink, working on his head would be easy. She still had to decide on a stunning background, although a part of her also considered leaving it blank so nothing distracted from his image. But before making a final decision, she wanted to hear Juan's opinion.

At his front door, Lina was greeted by Ervin, who gave her her daily dose of doggy love when she picked him up.

"You're getting big," she said, amazed at how rapidly he was growing. "Carrying you is becoming quite the workout."

Juan rounded the corner with a smile on his face —and a shirt on his back. Well, a tailored suit to be exact.

The unexpectedness of his get-up rendered her speechless for a moment. Part of her wanted to undress him, and the other part wanted him to do all kinds of kinky things to her.

"Wow, look at you, I almost didn't recognize you

with your clothes on." Her voice came out huskier than intended.

His gaze sharpened and heated.

Lina, clutching Ervin—her furry security blanket—stepped back as Juan approached. He took the puppy from her and set him down before backing her against the wall.

He traced her lip with his thumb and then gave her a kiss so passionate it made her momentarily forget her own name. His other hand found her butt and squeezed.

"I missed you," he said close to her ear in his sexy million-dollar voice.

They hadn't seen each other since he left for the movie premiere.

Lina tried to get her hands on his pants, but he caught her wrist.

"I have a meeting," he said and gave her another mind-scrambling kiss. "I'll see you later."

Lina remained leaning against the wall even after Juan closed the door behind him.

Daaang, that was hot. And anticlimactic.

"I guess it's just you and me now," she said to Ervin, who was pawing at her thighs.

The puppy followed her into the living room, where she helped him up onto the scaffolding. It had become their routine for him to curl up on a pillow by her feet and sleep while she painted.

She was going to miss the dog. What were the odds that Juan would give Ervin to her as a parting gift?

As she painted, Lina's thoughts drifted back to the

movie premiere. She'd been avoiding thinking about it and intentionally hadn't asked Juan how it went—whether he'd talked to her dad at all and how he seemed...

Dammit.

A hundred years could pass and she'd still be the young girl missing her dad. Tears welled up in her eyes, blurring her vision. She fought them back when Ervin's paw and then his cute little head landed on her foot, giving her silent comfort.

She crouched to stroke the puppy. "Thank you."

Lina painted throughout the afternoon and into the early evening until Juan texted her. His meeting was running late but she was welcome to stay the night if she wanted.

As tempted as she was to try out his massive bed, she also felt too vulnerable and therefore at risk to ask him about her dad.

Ervin wasn't pleased when it was time for her to leave, so she texted Juan that she had to go home to prep for a client meeting, and his dog would be coming with her for a sleepover at her place.

You little dog thief, he texted back. *See you tomorrow?*

I'll text you, she replied.

CHAPTER 6

Don't go breaking my heart

Meeting Manuel Campos was an unforgettable experience. They met at a country club in Mesa De Los Santos, a plateau in the Andes mountain range near the Chicamocha canyon, about forty minutes from Lina's house.

She hoped Manuel hadn't chosen the location for privacy, because, from staff to patrons, everyone stared at him or stopped him on his way over to the table Lina had chosen. What would've been a thirty-second walk across the room took him all of five minutes.

While she waited, Lina gazed out the panoramic window that overlooked the vast, tropical landscape. It was one of the reasons she loved living on the outskirts of Bucaramanga. The abundance of green was soothing to the soul: calming, restorative, and healthy.

"Lina, thanks so much for coming out here to meet me." Manuel's smooth voice drew her attention back to the present moment. He wore jeans and an emerald green T-shirt. His stubble was neatly trimmed, and his slightly curled hair added to his charm.

His smile was gorgeous too.

She stood to greet him, and they exchanged cheek kisses.

Manuel was about the same height as Juan, around 5'10", which was considered tall by Colombian standards. He was also in admirable shape, although not as brawny as Juan. Everything about him had a softer, less intimidating quality.

"It's not exactly a hardship," she said with a smile. "I'm living the dream, getting to meet the people I admire."

"Thank you, and ditto." He gestured for her to take a seat. "Your art is incredible."

"Thanks," she said, tucking her hair behind her ear. Also, wow. Crazy to be sitting here with one of her idols because *he* was a fan of *her* work. She shook her head to clear the daze. "Can you tell me more about what you'd like me to paint?"

Manuel wanted to donate a mural to a school. "These kids are remarkable, and I want this mural to reflect that." He took out his phone and showed her a rough collage of his ideas. Although it wasn't polished, she understood his vision.

Some of the children depicted in the collage were missing limbs, one was in a wheelchair.

Since 1990, landmines had caused the death or injury of almost 12,000 Colombians, making it the second-highest casualty rate after Afghanistan.

Lina was already a supporter of the cause, donating money to landmine clearance efforts each year.

She responded without hesitation. "I'll do it."

***

Two days later, Juan spilled his afternoon coffee when he came across a picture of Lina and Manuel Campos sitting close together in a restaurant. The headline proclaimed: *Colombian Pop Icon Manuel Campos Finds Romance with an Enigmatic Beauty, Leaving Fans Intrigued.*

"Hell no." Juan showed the article to Ervin, who lifted his head from his doggy bed and eyed him curiously. "Can you believe this, Erv?" Juan stretched his neck from side to side. "Damn, Campos. The girl is mine."

It was almost comical. The media had perpetuated a rivalry between him and Manuel over the years, but in reality, he'd never had an issue with the man and even enjoyed his music.

Ervin trotted over and sniffed the picture. "Don't give me that look," Juan said with a chuckle. "I know she's your girl too."

He got up from the armchair on his balcony and went downstairs to the living room, where Lina was engrossed in her work, finishing the back of his head. She didn't stop or turn around when he approached, and he didn't expect her to. When Lina was in her creative zone, she was one hundred percent focused, oblivious to everything else happening around her.

The house could be on fire and she probably wouldn't notice. It presented a unique challenge because the scaffolding was now so high, startling her could be fatal.

Despite being just a few feet away, Juan decided to text her instead of calling out to her.

Can you come find me when you take a break? I want to ask you something, he texted, knowing her phone wouldn't make a sound while she was working.

Lina startled him with her verbal response. "What's up?"

"Can you come down here for a moment?" Juan unlocked his phone as she made her way down.

When she stood in front of him, her beautiful smile—and the paint stain on her cheek—gave him a warm feeling in his chest.

"Hi," he said, a flush creeping up his neck.

"Hi." Lina pressed up onto her tiptoes and gave him a gentle kiss on the lips.

He sighed, his tone hesitant when he spoke. "You genuinely like me, right?"

Her smile dimmed by five degrees. "Nope. The only person in the world that I kiss is the one I don't like." She smacked his chest. "What is this really about?"

He showed her the gossip column, and Lina made a sound somewhere between a squeak and a cough. "This is not what it looks like." She stabbed at the screen. "They photoshopped the phone he was holding out of the picture. He was showing me a collage on his phone. I came closer because I wanted to see the details, not because I was going to hold his hand."

Juan reached out and ran his fingers up Lina's arm, igniting goosebumps. "If he asked you out, you'd say no?" he said, his voice tinged with curiosity and concern. "I'd rather you tell me now before I'm so in love with you it's going to break my heart."

Lina groaned theatrically. "As much as it pains me, all of me wants all of you."

In response, he peppered her neck and shoulder with kisses until Lina was squealing and shaking with laughter. Then he placed his hand on the back of her neck and captured her mouth with his.

The feeling of her body pressing into his was intoxicating, overpowering. He couldn't wait to lose himself in her.

The curious tangle of their tongues grew into a *champeta* dance that left them panting. As they kissed, he moved them towards the sofa where he lowered them onto the cushions. Lina's legs scissored around him, giving them both the connection they craved.

Just as he snaked his hand under her shirt, someone cleared their throat behind them—loudly.

Juan lowered his forehead to Lina's chest and took a deep breath. When he lifted his head, Lina had covered her eyes with her arm, but a smile played on her lips.

He leaned in and kissed her before addressing the interrupter. "Seriously, sis? Now? Do you know how long I've been waiting for this?"

Both Noelia and Lina chuckled, and Juan moved off Lina, offering her a hand to help her sit up. "No, meet Angelina. Lina, meet my sister Noelia."

Lina greeted Noelia with a small wave and a warm smile. "Hi."

Noelia grinned as she took a seat on the sofa across from them. "Nice to finally meet you. You truly are a hot Mrs. Claus!"

Lina glanced at Juan, her bottom lip drawn into her mouth, her eyes twinkling with humor.

"When I hired you, I didn't know what you looked like. So No asked me if I would play 'Catching Santa.'"

Lina tilted her head to the side. "And did you?"

"I wanted to, but since we literally ran into each other, I didn't have to." Juan turned to Noelia and pointed behind her.

Noelia's mouth hung open in awe as she took a few steps toward the mural. "Holy shit, bro, this is incredible." She turned to Lina. "You're a genius!" Then she looked back at Juan and added, "You should've paid her more. I've never seen anything like this."

Juan placed his hand over Lina's ankle to get her attention. "I hope you're going to raise your prices after this."

Resting her forehead against her palms, Lina propped her elbows on her knees. "The price of art is highly subjective. Just because you think you'd pay that much doesn't mean others would too."

"You've seen my house. I know a thing or two about

the value of art, so I feel confident saying I'm not the only one who'd pay a premium for your work. This is a showstopper piece," he said, gesturing toward the mural.

Lina sighed. "Maybe I will. Thanks to your unsolicited marketing, I now have a long waitlist to work through."

"You deserve it." Juan put his arm around her and kissed her temple. He felt a surge of pleasure when Lina placed her hand on his thigh.

Noelia gestured between the two of them. "So, are you two officially an item now?"

"Are we?" he asked Lina.

"Exclusive, yes. But official? I'm not ready to be scrutinized by the media. I still have a bad aftertaste from earlier, so let's keep this between us for now."

Fair enough.

Noelia's eyes widened in curiosity. "What happened earlier?"

Juan showed the article to his sister.

Noelia's gaze remained fixated on the picture of Lina and Campos. "Whoa. I can't blame you, Lina. That's one attractive man."

Juan playfully shoved his sister. "You're supposed to be on my side."

Noelia shrugged. "Yeah, but you're my brother. I refuse to see your hotness. To me, you're still toothless and wearing diapers."

Lina couldn't contain her laughter and covered her face with her hands. "I can see why you keep her around."

Juan's phone rang on the coffee table, and to his surprise, it was Lin-Miguel Santos calling. Lina had likely glimpsed the caller ID too, as she became almost eerily still.

Juan picked up the phone and stepped outside to take the call.

"I'm pretty sure Lina saw you calling me," he greeted Lin-Miguel.

"Better me than her dad. Listen, we have to move up the meeting. Do you think you can convince her to go to Miami with you this weekend?"

"If I ask her now, she'll be suspicious."

"Then the weekend after. In the meantime, make sure she stays away from Manuel Campos."

"Okay..." Juan said, to himself, as the line went dead. Not cryptic at all. He didn't think Campos had a bad reputation.

The plot thickens, he thought to himself but remembered he was smart enough not to dictate who Lina could or couldn't hang out with.

Trust was essential in their relationship. She had chosen him, and he chose to trust her. Next weekend would be better anyway, as by then she would likely be done with the mural and he could take her to Miami to celebrate. Hopefully without any interruptions from people or pets during crucial moments.

CHAPTER 7

Tabloid rumors &
surprise guests

It was only a couple of days later when Lin-Miguel called again. Juan stepped out of the shower, cursing as a drop of water dripped onto his special-edition iPhone.

"Yo, what's up?" he said in greeting as he wrapped a towel around his lower half, the phone clamped between his ear and shoulder.

"I saw the new pictures." Lin-Miguel's voice held a tinge of urgency. "Whatever you're doing, it's not working."

Juan sat on the edge of his bed and put the phone on speaker so he could finish drying off. "What are you talking about?"

"Lina and Campos. You need to put an end to this. I don't care how you do it, but they can't be together."

"I can assure you they aren't together."

"The pictures tell a different story. How can you be so calm about this? I thought you liked her."

He was calm because Lina told him nothing was going on between her and Campos, and he chose to believe her.

"Are you any closer to getting her to Miami?" Lin-Miguel asked, again with an urgency that made Juan think he was missing something.

"Yes, she's almost done with the mural, so I'm taking her there to celebrate."

After they hung up, Juan asked Siri to show him the latest news on Manuel Campos. His chest tightened when he saw the most recent pictures of Manuel and Lina.

This time the headline read, *Stepping Out in Style: Manuel Campos and Mystery Lady's Cozy Outing Leaves Fans Wondering!*

One of the pictures showed the two of them hugging each other. Lina wore reddish-brown suede heels, light-wash jeans that frayed at the hem, and a long woolen cardigan with the sleeves pushed up. The color was similar to her shoes, but it had a bold black pattern on it resembling Xs.

Campos was dressed in jeans and a checkered short-sleeve button-down over a band T-shirt.

They did look stylish—and cozy.

The other picture showed Campos loading a box into the trunk of a car, and Lina standing next to him, smiling. The last picture was of Campos holding the car door open for her, and this time he was smiling at her.

Lina chose that moment to join Juan on the bed. She sat behind him and let her hands travel over his shoulders and down his pecs. It felt incredible, but he knew it wouldn't last because he was still holding the phone with her and Campos's picture on display.

As predicted, her hands stilled, and then she grabbed the phone before he could turn off the screen.

"I was wondering why you seemed so tense," she said, handing him back the phone.

"This time *you* have to trust me that this is not what it looks like."

Her rigid posture softened. "Then what are you doing?"

Juan debated for a moment what he should tell her.

In the end, he went with the truth. "Your godfather made it sound like Campos isn't a safe person for you to be around. He asked me to make sure you two don't spend time together—"

"What? Why?"

"He didn't say why, but it seemed important. Why are you spending time with Campos anyway? You said you weren't interested in him."

"He hired me to paint a mural for a school. The students are victims of landmines. Manuel and I get along on a personal level, which is why he offered to help me get the supplies from my studio. That's what's happening in the pictures."

She gestured at his phone. "Nothing about him gives me a weird feeling. If I were unsafe with him, I'd sense something."

Juan nodded, then slumped backward onto the

mattress and rubbed his palms against his temples. "I don't know why Lin-Miguel wants to protect you from Campos, and I also don't know what to do because I want to let you do your thing, but I also don't want you to get hurt."

Lina straddled his hips and stroked her hands over his abs and pecs before resting them on his shoulders. Then she leaned down and kissed him with a tenderness that expanded his chest. "Do you think if I unfasten your towel, some kind of alarm will go off?"

He chuckled. "Don't jinx it."

Lina grasped the hem of her tank top and pulled it off over her head. She wore a black lace bralette with embroidered black roses covering her nipples.

Juan ran his fingertips over the thin fabric before he cupped her breasts. A generous handful as he'd thought. "You are so beautiful."

Lina removed her hand from his left shoulder and stroked over his chest before placing her palm over his heart. "So are you. You're my favorite subject to paint so far."

Juan pushed up from the mattress so Lina was sitting in his lap. He found her lips with his.

And then the phone rang.

They both groaned.

"Let's pretend it's music," he mumbled against her lips, but Lina broke the kiss and craned her neck.

"It's my goddamn godfather again! I swear..." She reached for his phone, but Juan clasped her wrist.

"You're going to say something you'll regret. Let

me talk to him."

The phone stopped ringing.

A couple of seconds later, a text message lit up the screen. Juan picked it up and read the message aloud. "Change of plans. Convince Lina to stay with her at her place and don't let her out of your sight."

Juan shook his head and pressed the callback button, but the call went straight to voicemail. He let out a frustrated sigh before directing his gaze at Lina. "What do you want to do?"

"This is very bizarre."

"Sure is."

Lina threw her hands in the air. "I guess we're going to my place, and you can babysit me, but Erv is coming with us."

She strutted out of the room and called over her shoulder, "Get ready. I'll meet you at my place. I'll text you the address."

"No. I'll follow you in my car. Remember the 'don't let her out of your sight' part?"

"Fine. I'll wait in the car."

***

This was stupid, Lina thought on her way over to her house. Manuel Campos wasn't dangerous. There must be a different explanation. Maybe it was about the media coverage? Could Manuel have a stalker who wanted to get rid of her because she was his rumored girlfriend?

Traffic between their private roads was all but nonexistent, so Juan was behind her for the entire ten-minute drive. Her estate was more modest in size but still, a beautiful, spacious place to live.

Lina opened the gate, waiting for Juan to pass through before closing it behind them.

Her bungalow was a contemporary build with natural wood siding and large black-framed windows. The flatter roofline gave it a slightly Japanese vibe.

Her home had all the rooms she could ever need. Three bedrooms and three bathrooms. A study, a workout room, one expansive living room, and a state-of-the-art kitchen. Her atelier was in the pool house, so she could use the natural light and find inspiration in the breathtaking landscape.

Since Ervin already knew her place, the puppy ran over to the cushioned bench by the window, where he curled up and basked in the sunlight.

"I see Erv already feels at home." Juan set down his duffel bag and the dog's stuff. The entrance hall had a big skylight that let in even more light. "Your home is beautiful and cozy," he said, looking around, "calming more than anything."

Where the interior of Juan's house was bright white with marble floors, hers had a more natural feel to it. A couple of walls were exposed brick, and the floors were recycled hardwood and tile. Her furniture was mostly mid-century modern, whereas his was more contemporary.

The funny thing was that *she* was the artist, but she had way fewer artworks in her home than Juan had in his. What she did have in abundance were plants of all shapes, colors, and sizes: crotons with their multicolored leaves, heliconias with their deep red lobster claws, and of course, a great variety of orchids, Colombia's national flower.

Lina led him into the living room, which did have a mural of her own design: native plants with a blue-green butterfly.

The accent wall behind the arched bookcases caught his eye. She had painted colorful palm trees and jungle plants on a black background. "Have you ever thought about turning some of your designs into wallpapers or selling reprints of some of your paintings?"

She had thought about making her art more widely accessible, so she could have a passive revenue stream in case she didn't want to or couldn't paint anymore. "That's basically my retirement plan. I just haven't gotten around to figuring out the logistics."

"If you ever need an investor, I'm in."

She blew him a kiss before she headed into the kitchen. Juan followed her. He was taking that whole 'not letting her out of his sight' order way too seriously. The tension bouncing off him put her on edge too.

She stopped in the center of the kitchen, the island between them. "Should we just have sex? This tension is making me crazy."

He scowled at her.

Got it. Apparently not.

The doorbell rang, signaling someone at the gate.

Lina raised her eyebrows at Juan, who shrugged in response.

"What do you want to do?" he asked, scanning their surroundings.

"Let me check the camera." Lina took out her phone and opened the app, with Juan peering over her shoulder.

He growled. "What's he doing here?"

Lina pressed the button to open the gate, and the car passed through.

She walked outside when the car pulled up in front of the entrance.

As the window rolled down, Manuel looked at her with furrowed brows. "W-why are you here?"

"What's going on?" she asked, rubbing her temple.

"I... I'm here for a meeting? I didn't know you'd be here."

"A meeting? Did you talk to my godfather?"

"Your godfather?"

"Lin-Miguel Santos?"

"I was supposed to meet him here. I thought this was his place... Didn't know you had any relation to him. He told me to stay away from you because you're not who I think you are. So did my mother... I don't understand why you're here."

Lina wrapped her arms around herself. "I live here, and he said the same thing to me about you. He isn't even here. The only one who is here is..." She peered over her shoulder, but Juan wasn't there.

"None of this makes sense," she muttered to herself. "I'm starting to freak out."

"Yeah, me too."

For a moment, they stared at each other.

"What do we do now?" Lina could sense that Manuel didn't want to get out of the car, and she felt rooted to the ground.

She jumped when Juan said her name from behind her.

Manuel's eyes widened. "You have Manolo at your house?"

She turned to face Juan, who looked poised for a fight with a scowl on his face, his palm covering his fist, accentuating his strained muscles. Dangerous yet ruggedly sexy. "Manuel, meet Juan. Juan, meet Manuel."

Neither of them said a word to each other.

"Um, do you want to come inside?" Lina asked Manuel, but she placed her palm on Juan's chest to calm him down as he made a low, threatening sound. "We can try to figure out together what Lin-Miguel is up to."

"Together as in the three of us?" Manuel asked.

"Do you have a problem with that?" Juan took a step closer. "I'm not leaving her alone with you until I'm convinced she's safe with you."

"Is he your boyfriend or something?" Manuel opened the car door, almost knocking it into Juan.

"Can we go inside?" Lina hooked her arm around Juan's and moved toward the entrance door, with Manuel following closely behind.

They had barely sat down to have coffee when Lin-Miguel burst into her living room. It was the person

coming after him that made Lina drop her cup,
which clattered onto the small plate, spilling coffee
onto the table.

CHAPTER 8

A surprise reunion

Lina didn't have time to process what was happening as Lin-Miguel immediately barked at her.

"Are you sleeping with him?"

Lina remained speechless. Of all the things her godfather could have said, he chose to lead with that? Could this day get any crazier?

With her heartbeat racing and a fluttery feeling in her belly, she fixed her gaze on her other unexpected guest.

In the middle of her living room stood her dad, worry etched on his face. He had a few more wrinkles around his eyes and forehead. Silver streaks ran through his dark hair, neatly trimmed beard, and mustache. Yet, aside from that, her dad still looked almost exactly like he did ten years ago.

"Sweetheart, it's important," was the first thing her dad said to her.

She peered down at the coffee pooling on her solid wood table. "That's personal. But if people would stop interrupting us, we would be having sex right now. So how about you get out of my house?"

Both her dad and Lin-Miguel scrubbed a hand over their mouths as if they had practiced the exasperated gesture.

"So did you?" her dad prompted, his eyes directed at Manuel.

Manuel squirmed in his seat. Leaning over to Lina, he said, "Why is he glaring at me?"

"Yes, Dad, why are you glaring at him?"

"I'm glad he's not glaring at me," mumbled Juan from her other side.

Lin-Miguel handed her dad his phone, which gave Lina deja vu from when Juan asked her about the pictures and showed them to Noelia.

"Dad, if this is what I think it is, then you've got this all wrong. I was talking about Juan," she said, jerking her thumb at him.

"Great, Lina, now he is glaring at me," muttered Juan.

"You're sleeping with my daughter?"

Both Lina and Juan sagged in relief when her dad said, "Oh thank God."

"That's not approval," Lin-Miguel stressed, "It's just better than the alternative."

"About that," said Manuel, "why did you tell us to stay away from each other?"

Juan slapped his thighs. "Oh my God, look at each other! Around the lips and the nose." He circled his hand in front of Lina's face. "You're related." He addressed the two men standing. "What is it, cousins, siblings?" He turned back to Lina and Manuel. "Definitely siblings—that's why they wanted to make sure you two didn't get it on."

Lina stared at Juan, then at Manuel, then at her dad. "Is-ah-is that true?"

"I'm pretty sure it is, Lina," Manuel said, bouncing his knee. "My mom was being weird too. I mean, she's always been protective, but when she saw the pictures of us, she almost fainted and wanted me to promise that I wouldn't talk to you again."

"Dad?"

"I'm sorry it's coming out like this, but yes, Manuel's mother and I had a one-night stand. Technically, she is your mother too."

"The mother who abandoned me as a newborn?" Lina choked out. Her head spun as she tried to catch her breath. "Out. All of you." She pressed her hands to the sides of her face and rocked back and forth. "Now."

All four men left the room.

Then the sobs came. She prodded her temples harder.

When Lina was ten, she tried to find out who her mother was. Her dad had told her he didn't know the woman. It was one night filled with so much *aguardiente* he could barely remember it. And when Lina asked for her birth certificate, he said it had gotten lost and they would figure out how to replace it when she wanted to get married.

After that, she'd asked for a paternity test to find out if her dad even was her dad. Instead of granting her request, he showed her old pictures of *his* mother, who looked so much like Lina. *"You're mine, sweetheart, and you'll always be mine."*

All she had ever known about her birth mother was her last name, Valencia, which was a very common name and therefore of no help in uncovering her identity.

Just when Lina felt like she couldn't breathe, she spotted movement out of the corner of her eye. Juan was on his knees, saying something to Ervin before the puppy came over to her and licked her face.

Juan got up and disappeared around the corner.

"Stay, please," she said but wasn't sure if he'd heard her.

A few seconds later, Juan walked back into the room and knelt in front of her. He gave Ervin a cuddle before he sent the puppy back to his favorite spot.

Lina let out a shaky breath when he wrapped his arms around her.

He held her for a long time.

Once she calmed down enough to talk, she sang, "You're amazing. I'm attracted. Let's have sex to get distracted."

He chuckled and kissed her forehead. "I'm sorry you have to deal with all of this, and I'm here for you, but I will never take advantage of you when you're in a state like this."

Lina moved her hands up to his handsome face. "How is it taking advantage if it's what I want? We would've already done it if it weren't for all the interruptions."

"Lina—"

"I'd get it if you had suggested it while I was in tears. But it was me, and I want—"

He interrupted her words with a soft but rousing kiss. The gentle way he guided her back onto the sofa, arranging a plush throw pillow to cradle her head, made her feel cared for.

As Juan's body covered hers, Lina released a contented sigh. "See, I'm feeling better already."

He gave her an affectionate smile before he lowered his mouth to her neck and teased her with hot licks and kisses, sending delicious tingles down to her toes.

Juan brought his arm under her and lifted her so the apex of her thighs nestled against his growing erection.

They both moaned when he thrust his hips.

Lina nipped his bottom lip and gave his glorious butt a squeeze. "Man, I've wanted to do this since you sent me your picture for the painting."

"And does it live up to your imagination?"

"Best ass I've ever seen or touched."

Grinning, he slid a hand under her top and pinched her nipple, making her buck against him.

As he scooted back, he pushed her top and the lace bralette up over her head, and let his heated gaze travel over her. "You're so damn gorgeous."

Lina sat up and slid her hands under his shirt, exploring the muscles there. His body truly was a work of art.

Juan gripped the back of his shirt and pulled it off, then embraced her so they were skin to skin.

"I love being close to you," she admitted.

He stroked her cheek and rested his forehead against hers. "It just feels right, doesn't it?"

Her throat grew thick, and with a nod, she brought her arms around his neck.

His lips brushed against hers. "Let's see if I can make you feel even better."

Juan lowered her back onto the cushion, then let his palms roam over her stomach and chest. Every time he grazed her nipple she felt the heat pool between her legs. She moaned his name when he replaced his hands with his mouth.

He topped the sensation when he slipped his fingers into her shorts and under her lace panties. Keeping his touch featherlight, he stroked her without hitting the spot where she craved him the most.

"Please."

He sucked her nipple into his mouth and circled her clit, lighting her body on fire.

She was so close to coming when he pulled away. "Hey!"

Juan smiled wickedly as he pulled her pants down, leaving her exposed to him. He flipped her over, squeezed one of her butt cheeks, and smacked the other. Then he helped her up onto her knees and she gripped the throw pillow hard when he stroked her with his tongue.

Again he brought her right to the edge of orgasm

only to pull away.

Lina heard some rustling and the ripping of foil.

Juan turned her around, and because she was still wet, the tip of his erection slid right into her. He went slow the last few inches, giving her time to adjust to the fullness.

Once he was completely inside her, they both smiled.

"We finally made it," she whispered before Juan gave her a long, glorious kiss.

"You feel so good," he murmured against the shell of her ear as he slid in and out with long slow strokes. "Touch yourself."

Lina caressed her breasts and then reached between them, closing her eyes as she savored the experience.

"So good," she panted as she met him with every thrust.

Urging her on, Juan pushed her leg up and moved the lumbar pillow under her butt, letting go when she held the position. Gripping her hip, he began to move faster, the new angle making every sensation, every stroke, more intense.

His breathing grew ragged too and they both came, holding on tight.

Juan kissed her deeply, and with each reassuring kiss, Lina fell a little more in love with him.

"I know your inclination is to run," he said, cradling her head. "But please try to trust that I want to stay with you, that I choose you."

Nodding amidst the tears welling in her eyes, Lina

felt the abandoned little girl inside her, still present even at twenty-five years old. "I need therapy," she confessed, tilting her head back in an attempt to hold in the tears.

One tear managed to escape despite her efforts. "I want to leave you so you can't leave me. That's how messed up I am," she said, covering her eyes with her arm. "I avoid relationships because I don't know what's going to happen. I might become too clingy or try to sabotage this to keep myself from getting attached."

Juan removed her arm and placed a kiss over her heart. "At least we know what we're dealing with."

"Why do you want to put yourself through this?" she asked, her voice trembling. "You're an attractive guy. You're charming and you're set financially. You have options."

"You're the option I want."

She shook her head. "Why?"

Her stomach fluttered when he gazed at her. She could see it in his eyes before he said it.

"I'm in love with you, Lina. That's why I'm sticking with you."

She pulled him into another kiss, pouring all her affection into it. "I feel it too."

"Yeah?" he said, almost shyly.

"Yeah."

His eyes drifted shut, and his features relaxed. Lina couldn't help but be struck by how captivating he was. She caressed his cheek, savoring this special moment with him.

Juan took her hand and pressed a kiss into her palm before wrapping her in his arms. There was nowhere else she'd rather be.

Inhaling against his warm skin, she silently expressed gratitude for his persistence and offered a prayer that her skittishness wouldn't deter him.

His presence felt nothing short of magical. The man radiated warmth and strength that she couldn't resist. And he wanted her, out of all people. That made her feel special too, because she knew he was selective about who he allowed into his life.

Juan's fingertips stroked up and down her back, making her sigh with contentment. It had been so long since someone had given her tenderness. Aside from her childhood, there had been no one. The other two encounters in her past hardly counted, though she credited the guys for being committed to her pleasure.

The sparks and butterflies she experienced with Juan were on a different level entirely. It was an attraction that felt visceral and bone-deep, a once-in-a-lifetime connection that was absolutely worth fighting for.

"Do you think you're going to talk to your dad while he's here?" Juan's question burst her romantic bubble.

Lina pinched the bridge of her nose. "You think he's going to stay here? He probably took the next flight home." Home. Not where *she* was, where his family was.

"He hasn't left," Juan assured her.

"How do you know?"

"You're his daughter, Lina. And he's lucky to have such an awesome kid like you. For all his faults, he knows that."

"I wish," she whispered, her throat tightening. Her dad had been the best, and it broke her heart all over again that he wasn't a part of her life anymore.

Juan disentangled himself from her and reached for his jeans, pulling out a scrap of paper. "He gave me this for you."

Her heartbeat quickened as she unfolded the paper and read her dad's note.

Sweetheart,
I'm sorry I upset you. I regret how I handled certain things, but I will never regret that one-night stand because it gave me you. I'm staying at Lin's place. I hope you come talk to me.
Love,
Dad

Her breath hitched as the emotions swamped her. Juan brought his arm around her and kissed her temple.

"Will you come with me?" she asked as she wiped her eyes.

"If that's what you want, I'll be there."

"I feel safe when I'm with you."

"You do?" Juan puffed out his chest and Lina chuckled.

She hugged his bicep and planted a kiss on his cheek.

His protectiveness was endearing, not stifling, showing her he cared. His mother had done a great job with him, Lina decided and considered sending the woman flowers or a painting of Juan and Noelia as a token of her appreciation for raising such remarkable kids.

"Let's go," he suggested.

"Now?" Lina coughed. "Why the rush?"

"Because you're still hopped up on love hormones." He gave her a kiss to prove his point. "The longer you wait, the more time you have to talk yourself out of it."

"Maybe part of me wants to wait and see if he'll stick around," Lina confessed.

Juan clasped her hand. "Can I give you some tough love?"

"If you must."

"You both need to put aside your pride for this to work. He already made the first step by reaching out to you. The ball's in your court now." When she nodded, he added, "And you have to call Campos at some point. I'm sure he's struggling with this too." After a moment, he said, "I wonder if his dad knows."

Manuel was her *brother*. How crazy was that? Who knew if he even wanted her in his life…

An incoming message interrupted her thoughts, and the lit screen of her phone held the answer.

Juan encouraged her to pick it up.

Lina drew back her shoulders and faced the message from her brother, which said: *Wow, brother and sister? How crazy is that? I've always wanted a sibling. I'm hoping we can talk later. I'm going to confront my mom. I don't get how she could hide this from me.*

Lina showed Manuel's text to Juan, who absentmindedly stroked her thigh as he read. "That's what really sucks about this whole thing," he muttered, giving her thigh a squeeze. "They robbed the two of you of so many years together. How much less lonely you would've been knowing you had a brother right here in this city..."

A wave of grief for all the things that could have been washed over her, tightening her chest and bringing forth more tears.

Juan pulled her against him, holding her until his warmth began to calm the warring emotions inside her.

"Your hugs are the best," she admitted with a hitched breath.

He laughed softly.

"I mean it. It's like being swaddled in a protective love cloud."

Now he was full-on laughing. "A love cloud?"

She patted his chest. "I don't know how to explain it, okay? It just feels really good."

He crushed his mouth to hers and pushed her back into the cushion.

When they had to break apart for air, she brushed her hands over his muscular back. "And you're the best kisser. I'm being spoiled."

"As flattered as I am, this is a two-way street. What you give is what you get. You are very easy to love."

That stunned her into silence and flooded her chest with a glow.

Juan smiled at her before he dropped another kiss on her lips and pulled her back into a sitting position. "Let's get dressed, otherwise we'll be here all night."

"I'll take the sex marathon, please."

He helped her up. "Under different circumstances, I'd be doing you in every way imaginable right now, but this is an opportunity to get your dad back. I know how much you miss him because every time I mention him, your face shows exactly how you feel."

CHAPTER 9

The long-overdue confrontation

They didn't speak during the twenty-minute ride to her godfather's estate. Lina could hardly keep from shaking in her seat. Thankfully, Juan was driving because, in her unstable state, she feared she would wrap the car around a tree.

As they arrived at the black iron gate, Lina felt herself close to hyperventilating. It only took a few seconds for the gate to open, and they drove up the long, tree-lined driveway to Lin-Miguel's sprawling mansion.

Juan was wealthy, but Lin-Miguel was likely the richest man around. He produced songs and movies that kids around the globe adored and replayed endlessly. His talent was unmatched.

She remembered fondly how he praised her own talent when she was a child, which helped boost her self-confidence in pursuing her art. While Lina hadn't spoken to her dad since she left Los Angeles ten years ago, Lin-Miguel had made an effort to stay in touch with her, respecting her decision to never discuss her dad.

Until his latest movie production. He'd shared with her that the script drew inspiration from their lives and that he wanted her dad to portray one of the characters. Not just any character, but the one resembling her—the one who had left the family under the impression that it was what they wanted.

She didn't think her dad would agree to it, as it would require him to put himself in her shoes, but to her surprise, he'd accepted the role. Deep down, Lina had hoped it would make her dad contact her, but he hadn't.

Juan parked the car and then took her hands in his. "Take slow, deep breaths," he instructed. "You've got this, okay?"

She nodded and followed his guidance, taking deep breaths as Juan climbed out of the car and opened the passenger door for her. She reached for his hand, and he pulled her into another comforting hug.

"You are the strongest woman I know. You'll be okay." He linked their hands and led her toward the entrance.

The massive wooden double door opened almost instantly.

Lina wasn't prepared for her dad to be the one greeting them. Her hand tightened around Juan's, and he spoke first because she couldn't find her words.

"Hey, John. Can we come in?"

We. Juan's choice of words spoke volumes. Knowing he was there with her gave her the strength to move.

Her dad gestured for them to take a seat in the informal sitting room.

While their houses were modern, Lin-Miguel's home was a traditional villa with red stone tiles and dark exposed wood beams. They sat in an olive green upholstered loveseat, and Juan held her hand on his thigh.

Her dad occupied the antique armchair across from them. "So you two are a couple?"

Lina nodded, and Juan asked, "Do you have a problem with that?"

Her dad rubbed the stubble on his chin. "When you have a daughter one day, you'll understand my hesitation."

Lina huffed. "Can't you just be happy for me? I wouldn't even be here if it weren't for him."

Her dad winced but then gave a determined nod.

Juan lightly squeezed her hand, and Lina released a long, calming breath.

Clearing his throat, her dad crossed and uncrossed his legs. "Do you think we can talk, just the two of us?"

Juan stood, and as her panic spiked, he reassured her, "I'll be down the hall, okay? Holler if you need me."

"He is a good man," she said when Juan had left the room. It was silly, but she still craved her dad's approval.

"I'm glad he treats you well, and I'm happy you're happy with him. But try to see it from my perspective too. You will always be my baby, and I will always be protective of you. Nothing will ever change that. Not distance, not time."

Hearing the words she'd longed to hear made tears well up in her eyes. She wanted to hug him, to break down the invisible barrier between them. Despite her efforts, the tears escaped. The surprising thing was that her dad's eyes were shiny too.

She didn't know who initiated it, but they met by the coffee table and fell into a tight embrace.

"I missed you so much," they both mumbled at once, sharing a teary laugh.

He held her against his chest and kissed the top of her head. Her dad was the original best hugger. That's why she loved Juan's hugs so much—they were as comforting as her father's.

"I'm so sorry I let you go. I've regretted it every damn day."

"Why didn't you stop me?" she said, biting back a sob.

"Because I didn't know what else to say or do to make you believe you were part of the family. I realized too late that I should've included Samantha in my relationship with you from the beginning. But like I said, you were my baby. I've always wanted to protect you, and maybe I tried to overcompensate for you growing up without your mother."

He rubbed her arms gently before guiding her back

onto the loveseat. "Sam told me once how difficult it was for her that I always kept you to myself. She was pregnant with Valeria at the time, crying and asking me if I would even be able to love our child the way I loved you."

He pressed the heels of his palms against his forehead, his eyes becoming misty once again. "I love all three of you kids so much, but the uncomfortable truth is my relationship with you will always be more intense because of what we've been through together. You were my first baby, and such a bright light during a time when I was struggling in every imaginable way."

Lina took his large hand in hers. "You were the best dad I could've asked for. It's not your fault my birth mother chose to abandon me. I never held that against you."

She sniffed and blinked at the ceiling before returning her gaze to her dad. "But I can't deny that her abandonment messed me up on a fundamental level. I always have this underlying feeling that something is wrong with me."

Squeezing her eyes shut for a moment, she let out a shaky breath. "That's the one thing I think you could've done—you should have put me in therapy with all the ways I acted out when Sam came into our lives."

He nodded solemnly. "Therapy wasn't part of our culture, and I believed we should work through our issues as a family. Times are different now, and if I could go back in time, I would've sought professional help for us. Sam actually pushed me into marriage counseling because of my behavior after you left."

As messed up as it was, it reassured her that their separation affected him too.

"Did the counselor ever tell you to reach out to me?"

Her dad didn't answer right away, hanging his head before looking at her again. "You were really hoping I would come for you, huh?"

She pulled her lips into her mouth, a fresh bout of tears threatening to fall. In a small voice, she said, "You are my dad."

"I'm so sorry, sweetheart," he said, tightening his hold on her hand. "I didn't know. I was hoping, but I didn't know. You were so angry and determined, you told me you never wanted to see any of us again."

"Because I was a hormonal teenager, Dad! Sure, I did mean it in that moment because it gave me autonomy in a situation where I felt I didn't have any. But I grew up with the belief that it would always be you and me against the rest of the world. Of course, I waited for you."

"And I didn't come."

"You didn't come."

Neither of them spoke after that. It was the rustling of Juan's return a few minutes later that cut through the thick cloud of emotions surrounding them.

Juan sat on the solid mahogany coffee table. He was misty-eyed too when he spoke. "Neither of you can change what has already happened, as painful as it is. But there's still so much love between you two. I hope you realize that if you don't reconcile it'll be your greatest regret."

Her dad was the first to find his voice. "Man, he really is a good man."

A small laugh bubbled out of her. "How did I get so lucky?"

Her dad's eyes were bright and glossy. "Because you're an incredible person, kid. I bet he's feeling pretty lucky too."

Juan shot her an 'I told you' look.

All three of them smiled.

"How long are you in town for?" Juan asked her dad while lightly stroking her forearm.

"I told my wife I have to make things right with my kid before I can leave."

The love Lina felt was almost as overwhelming as the pain she had experienced before.

"What did she say?" Juan posed the question Lina was too afraid to ask.

"'About time' is what she said," her dad replied, tugging at his shirt. "Samantha always knew we were a package deal and that being apart must be torture." He looked directly at Lina. "Everyone knows you got your stubborn streak from me. It's a heavy hitter when we direct it at other people, but it would create an inevitable impasse if we ever directed it at each other. That's what my therapist said."

Her eyes widened. "You have a therapist?"

"I have a therapist. I've got issues too. And a mountain of guilt to chip away at."

"I need to find one too," she admitted, tightening her hand into a fist, and then loosening it. If her dad had the courage to do therapy despite his cultural beliefs, she could do it too. "I'll sabotage my relationship with him if I don't." She pointed a thumb in Juan's direction.

All three of them went quiet until Juan gave her a playful pinch. "Let's head over to my place and celebrate this long overdue reunion."

"What about Ervin?" she asked because the puppy was still at her place.

Her dad's eyebrows furrowed. "Who's Ervin?"

"He's my baby." Juan placed a hand over his heart before he reached out to touch Lina's knee. "Though let's be real, at this point, he's as much hers as he is mine. You raised a little dog thief, John."

Her dad chuckled, and she perked up.

"Does that mean I can keep him?"

"Oh no. You can have partial custody, but that's it."

Her dad eyed them both with a headshake. "Let's hope you two will never break up. That's going to be a shit show."

"No, it won't." With a set jaw, Lina pushed her shoulders back. "We live only a ten-minute drive apart."

"I was hoping you would move back to L.A."

Her dad's wish left her speechless for a moment. She didn't dare look at the other man she loved. *Loved*, not just liked. "Juan is here, Dad. My studio is here. My house. And Ervin. My life is here now."

Her dad sighed. "I understand, even though I want you near me too. We've lost so many years."

"We can visit each other and talk on the phone. We can be in each other's lives without living together. You have an adult daughter, and like all parents of adult children, you need to let me navigate my life on my own."

"And she's very capable—that's a testament to you being her dad." Juan softened the blow. "Let's get going. My family can't wait to meet you two. We'll pick up Erv on the way."

CHAPTER 10

*Not your average
family gathering*

Her dad had to make a call but assured them he would meet them later at Juan's place. On their way back, Lina asked Juan to drop her off at her house, as she wanted to freshen up and use her own car.

The idea of meeting Juan's parents heightened her already anxious nerves. What if his mom didn't like her?

Lina slapped her cheeks, reminding herself that not every mother would reject her by default, despite her past experiences.

As much as she wanted to spend more time with her dad, seeing her stepmother again filled her with dread. Lina had said hurtful things to her before leaving, which made it even more surprising that Samantha had encouraged her dad to reconcile.

Sam wants to see her husband happy, she told herself, grateful that her dad had a caring partner in his life.

Staring at herself in the mirror, Lina had to resist the urge to cake on makeup to conceal the signs of her emotional twenty-four hours. Instead, she opted for her minimal routine, aware that she might burst into tears again and the raccoon-eyed look wouldn't be flattering.

Next on the agenda was her wardrobe. She cursed as she rummaged through her options, determined to make a good impression on Juan's parents since it was one of the few things she had control over. Except she had no clue what to wear, and collapsed onto the Moroccan pouf in her walk-in closet, burying her head in her hands.

Her phone buzzed in her pocket.

"Hey."

"You okay?" The tenderness in Juan's voice stirred a swarm of butterflies in her stomach.

"Mm-hm." She sighed. "I'm in the closet, trying to find the perfect 'hi, I hope it's okay I'm dating your son' outfit."

The phone beeped, indicating Juan's video call request. She took a deep breath before accepting.

The affection in his gaze nearly melted her. "They're going to love you, Lina. Just be yourself."

"I physically can't," she protested. "This is one of the few things I can control in this situation. I have to get this right."

To his credit, Juan didn't try to dismiss her concerns. "Show me what you have in mind."

"Okay, but promise me you won't choose based on what you find sexy, but rather what your mother would approve of."

"Under one condition." He smirked. "I get to choose what you're wearing underneath."

"If you say 'nothing,' I'm hanging up," she threatened, trying to suppress a smile.

"As much as I like that option, I can't sport a boner around our parents." His attempt at lightening the mood made her wish she could kiss him through the phone. "Let's opt for something less enticing."

With a smile, Lina presented the first option: a short but high-waisted black denim skirt and a camel-colored crew neck shirt with chunky rolled-up cap sleeves.

"The color suits you, and the outfit is classic and safe, but it lacks personality. What else do you have?"

She revealed a vintage antique-white silk top with spaghetti straps. The crop top had a flowy, uneven lace hem and intricate flowers stitched onto the bottom half. "It used to belong to my grandmother. Since it's such a statement piece, I would pair it with simple skinny jeans."

"Go with that one. My mom appreciates that kind of style, and the history behind the top shows your connection to family."

"Thanks." She blew him a kiss. "I'll be there in fifteen."

"Can't wait."

She groaned after they ended the call. He hadn't chosen her underwear. Since the top's triangular neckline didn't allow for a bra, she went with pasties.

In the end, it was the memory of how Juan had looked at her in the black lace getup that made her decide to wear a delicate Brazilian thong—a tiny black lace triangle covering the crotch, held together by three thin side straps.

***

Lina arrived at Juan's place half an hour later. She hesitated at the door, but Juan opened it not even thirty seconds later, pulling her into a kiss before she could get a word out.

As his lips moved against hers, her racing thoughts came to a soothing halt. He knew how to occupy her senses: roaming hands, enticing words, his fresh scent.

When he broke the kiss, he leaned his forehead against hers and hooked a finger under the waistband of her jeans.

"I want to see what you chose," he said, making her smile. "How about we take a quick detour upstairs?"

She stepped back and propped her hands on her hips. "Get your mind out of the gutter, Juan. We're here for serious business. Is my dad here?"

When he shook his head, a ball of anxiety rolled into her gut.

"He'll come." Juan ushered her inside and down the hall to his living room, where his parents and sister sat on the couch, chatting animatedly.

"Yo," he hollered to get their attention. "I'd like you to meet Lina. Lina, this is my mom, Maria Gaitana, and my dad, Lorenzo Peláez. You've already met No."

All three of them stood to kiss her cheek.

"We're so excited to finally meet you." His mom invited Lina to sit next to her, which felt like a promising start.

She didn't know much about Juan's parents except that they were divorced but had managed to remain civil. They were about her dad's age, and within minutes it became evident that they were just as charming as their kids. All three of them joked with her like they were old friends, allowing her to relax for the first time in days.

Despite the tempting presence of a bottle of *aguardiente*, Colombia's national drink, which Lina had brought as a gift, she chose to stick with water. Her worry over her dad not showing up bore the risk that she would drink more than she should.

With impressive timing, Lorenzo said, "Juan mentioned your dad will be joining us."

In response, her mouth went too dry to speak.

"He'll be here soon," Juan said with conviction. At least one of them believed in miracles.

As the minutes ticked on, Lina's anxiety grew. She could hardly keep her focus on the conversation.

When she didn't hear a question that was directed at her, Juan repeated, "He is going to come. He's running late because he had to take care of something first."

His family averted their eyes at what must have been a weirdly intense exchange. Was it too early to reveal her abandonment issues to them?

Thankfully, she didn't have to open her mouth

because the doorbell rang.

The relief that rushed through her system when her dad appeared in the living room made her want to lie down. This day was too much of a rollercoaster. She couldn't wait to sleep for twelve hours straight.

They all stood with their mouths hanging open.

Lina's gaze swayed from her dad to Juan's family and back to her dad.

"Star-struck," Juan whispered to her.

In her exhaustion, she'd forgotten that her dad was a famous movie star. "You didn't tell them who he is?"

"Nope." Grinning, he took a picture of his slack-jawed family.

His mother fanned herself with a magazine. "I love your movies."

"You know you have to marry her now," Noelia said to Juan with a wink at Lina. "*Mamá* won't let you mess up her chance to have her favorite actor as part of her family."

Juan, unfazed by his sister's comment, wrapped his arm around Lina's waist and kissed her temple. To her surprise, the thought of marrying him ignited a spark of excitement in her chest.

"Sorry I'm late. I had to pick up a surprise on the way." Her dad jutted his chin in the direction of the foyer.

Lina shifted her gaze toward the hallway, praying that this surprise would be less overwhelming than the previous ones.

The room erupted in excitement when Manuel Campos, Colombia's beloved heartthrob, strolled into the room.

Traces of tears and exhaustion dimmed his usual handsome appearance, and his smile appeared strained as if it took tremendous effort.

Lina's dad clapped Manuel on the shoulder, a sweet and reassuring gesture that softened her brother's features. "I'm sorry the three of us look like we've been through the wringer, but it's been an emotional day for us."

"Don't worry about it," María said with an understanding nod. "Juan prepared us that this might turn into an intense gathering."

Juan gave Lina a gentle push toward her father. She stumbled right into his arms, leaving tear stains on his shirt. The same happened when her dad passed her along to her brother. She got his shirt wet too, but when she peered up at his face, she saw his eyes were watery too.

"Let's step outside for a moment." She pulled Manuel out of the room by the sleeve of his Henley shirt. She led him to the front porch, where they settled into swinging chairs. There was nothing better than being rocked back and forth to find a sense of calmness.

"It's been quite the day." Lina offered a gentle smile.

Manuel nodded, absentmindedly rubbing his lip with his index finger.

They continued to rock as they gazed out into the distance.

After a while, Lina gathered the courage to ask, "Did you confront your mother?"

Manuel nodded again but avoided looking at her.

Her stomach formed a tight ball. "Didn't go so well?"

CHAPTER 11

A night to remember

It took her brother a full minute to tell her about his confrontation with his mother, and by that time, Lina was chewing on her cuticle to bear the tension.

Manuel's hands were restless too. "My dad didn't know."

Shit. Given the profound impact this news had on her, she dreaded even the thought of what it must have felt like for his dad to learn this about someone he'd loved and believed he knew so well for years.

Lina turned away and started picking at her nail. "I'm so sorry."

"It's not your fault." Manuel's gruff tone made her gaze dart back to him. "It happened during the early stages of my parents' relationship. She managed to hide it because she had relocated to Miami for work, while he continued to live and work in Bucaramanga for the first two years."

Shaking his head, he said, "I can't believe she did this to you—to us."

The realization that a single person's decision held the power to alter the course of numerous lives was truly startling. And a valuable lesson.

Manuel raked his hands through his hair before he folded his arms over his stomach. "At least you have an amazing dad. He talked to me before we got here, that's why we're late."

"I thought he wouldn't come, that's how messed up I am."

"That's what Juan said to us when we arrived. Not that you're messed up, of course, but that your dad being late triggered you. John told him he would be more mindful of that in the future."

Knowing Juan had her back injected her with a solid dose of dopamine.

"I like that you have someone who cares so much about you," Manuel said, pressing his fingers to his smiling lips. "He's so different from how he comes across in his videos."

A flush crept up her cheeks. "I never thought my first relationship would be with a guy like him. Famous like my dad, bad boy looks, and a total charmer... He's amazing though, kind and funny. And family matters to him."

The front door opened, and the man in question appeared in their line of sight.

"You guys doing okay?" Juan asked as he joined Lina and Manuel on the front porch.

"We were just talking about you," she said, biting back her smile.

"Do I want to know?"

"She gushed about you being a handsome devil," Manuel said with a mischievous grin.

So that's what it was like to have a brother close to her in age. "I didn't. Or at least not in those exact words," she corrected when Manuel snorted.

Juan pinched the front of his shirt. "What can I say, I'm a sexy beast." He took a step toward her and bent down to place a quick kiss on her lips. "Want to come back inside and have dinner with us?"

Manuel rubbed at his eyelid, his mouth opening and closing. "I never thought there would be a universe in which my sister is dating my alleged rival."

"*Alleged*. I don't have a problem with you. I don't know where the media got that bullshit."

"Same here. But hey, that kind of fabricated drama probably helped us sell albums." It was the next sentence that made Lina's chest constrict once more. "My mother can't see the difference between fact and fiction though. She's not a fan. I'm not proud of it, but in my anger, I threw it in her face that you two are together."

Juan's jaw ticked, but he didn't say anything.

"Good thing she has no say in my love life." Lina reached for Juan's hand to get out of the chair, and then did the same for her brother.

The rest of the night went off without a hitch. They opened the bottle of *aguardiente* and conversation flowed easily. Juan held Lina's hand as her dad entertained them with stories from her childhood. Memories of countless happy times flooded her mind, reminding her that there were far more cherished moments than she had thought.

It was past midnight when Lina was alone with Juan.

"How are you holding up?" he asked, leaning against the closed entrance door.

"I'm still standing—barely." When she swayed, Juan gripped her hips and drew her closer to him. "I'm absolutely, irrevocably in love with you, Juan Fernando Peláez Gaitana."

He kissed her with a passion that took her breath away. His fingers stroked down her arm and stomach, but she stopped his hand when he attempted to get under her top.

His burning gaze fanned her own desire. "Too much?"

Her fingers tingled with the need to touch him. "I don't want to stop. It's just that what I'm wearing underneath isn't sexy or what you'd expect."

Curious, he lifted her top and raised his brows. "How do we take it off?"

"Pull it off," she said, biting her lip. She did it herself though because it was without a doubt unsexy. "The bottom will make up for it, I promise."

When he opened the button of her pants and undid the zipper, he whistled in approval. "I'll be taking this off with my teeth."

"I expect nothing less." Lina stepped out of her jeans once he managed to pull them down. Goose bumps spread across her skin as he kissed her hip bone. The sight of him kneeling before her made her feel powerful and wanted.

As promised, he grasped the strings of her panties with his teeth and pulled them down. Not all the way, but enough to create a gap between the lacy fabric and her skin. She throbbed with need when he tilted his head and sucked the lace into his mouth, pulling her panties off and tasting her in the process.

Lina stood against the wall wearing nothing but the vintage top and a dangling gold necklace.

Juan spread her thighs farther apart, and then his fingers did the same with her folds as he thrust his tongue into her and licked a trail up to her most sensitive spot. When her hips bucked, he repeated the sweet torture until she was panting and pressing her fingers into the wall. She came hard, moaning his name through her climax.

Grasping her hips, Juan swiveled her around so she stood with her front facing the wall. He fondled her butt before he picked a condom from his pocket.

One of his hands found her hip and the other snaked under the front of her top, finding her breast. On a groan, he tightened his grip and pushed into her, inch by glorious inch, his breath hot against her neck.

He moaned when she contracted her muscles around him, his fingers teasing her nipple as he pulled out and slammed back into her, pushing her pelvis into the cool wall with each thrust.

"Turn around."

She did as she was told, watching him as he removed the condom and stroked his erection.

"Crouch with your legs apart."

She held the challenging position, her back firmly pressed against the supporting wall.

"Stroke yourself the way you like it."

She did until she was panting and delirious.

Juan strolled toward her with hunger in his eyes. When he reached her, he tilted her chin.

"Open for me, babe."

She took him into his mouth and tongued his length as he thrust in and out, his movements becoming sloppy as she brought him closer and closer to the edge.

"Lina," he moaned as he came, pressing his fingers into her scalp. "Make yourself come."

It took just a few more strokes before she followed, her legs trembling.

Juan grabbed a tissue from the console table and drew her into his arms. Since her legs had turned to jelly, he carried her upstairs to his bedroom— or straight to heaven because that's what it felt like when he put her down on his giant cloud-like bed.

"I'm never getting up again," she declared, grateful for her decision to forego the makeup earlier. As she burrowed into Juan's pillow, she closed her eyes with a satisfied sigh.

CHAPTER 12

Date night with a twist

When Lina woke up the next morning, a smile spread across her face. Juan was sitting propped up against the pillows, reading something on his phone while running his fingers through Ervin's soft fur.

Noticing she had opened her eyes, the puppy came over and licked her cheek.

"Seriously, Erv?" Juan scolded him. "I was going to be the one to kiss her awake!"

"It's not too late." She closed her eyes and pretended to snore.

Juan's laugh had the same effect as listening to her favorite song. The sheets rustled, and then he was on her, kissing her tenderly.

"How are you feeling?"

"So much better." She covered her yawn with the back of her hand. "What time is it?"

"Noon."

"What?" She had been joking about sleeping for twelve hours straight.

"You needed it." He stroked her arm, sending goosebumps across her skin.

"I thought you'd be busy today."

"I am. I took a break."

It was at that moment that she noticed Juan's outfit. He wore jeans and a fitted navy polo shirt with a red and white stripe down the front. He had an appreciation for fashion, just like her, although their styles differed. His taste leaned towards the eccentric, embracing bold patterns and vibrant colors, while she gravitated towards an autumn palette, blending her classic style with locally sourced artisanal pieces.

"Want to go on a date with me tonight?" he asked, his smile as radiant as the sunshine filtering through the window.

"A date? Like going to a restaurant?" She wasn't fond of the classic date idea but willing to do it.

"Yeah, or, you know, something less cliché and boring." He chuckled when she perked up.

"What did you have in mind?"

He scratched at the scruff on his jaw. "Sunset hike near Las Gachas and then stargazing in a hot spring. Or, we could dress up fancy and go to an art show."

"Man, I like both options."

He gave her a swift kiss. "You have all afternoon to decide. I have a Zoom interview in five."

Lina cuddled with Ervin for a few more minutes before she picked up her phone and checked the art show options. Maybe they could go to that first and then do the hike? If they didn't go when everyone else would be there they could minimize the attention.

The prospect of stepping out with Juan in public made her heart beat faster, and not in a good way. She had already gotten a preview of what it would be like when she met with her brother, and for some reason, she had a feeling it would be even more intense with Juan.

Her dad had always kept her out of the public eye, so all the famous people she'd met over the years were just people to her. She never thought she'd end up dating one of them.

As the clock neared five, Lina felt inclined to pretend she had a headache so they could stay in. Curling up on one of the extendable loveseats in his theater room sounded much more appealing with each passing minute. Thankfully, Juan was still working, so he didn't pick up on her lack of enthusiasm.

You made a commitment, she chided herself as she walked into the kitchen to prepare them a snack. She'd gone home earlier to pick out her outfit and bring a suitcase of clothes and toiletries back to his place.

Juan had been very direct with her about his plans going forward. Because he would be gone for long stretches of time when he went on tour, he wanted them to stay together when he was home, whether it be at his place or hers.

They both agreed that they would rather go all in now and see if it worked out, rather than going slow and wasting both of their time.

The truth was, they led an unconventional life, so it made sense that a timeline that worked for most couples wouldn't be ideal for them. She didn't even want to think about him being gone for months on end, and thankfully they still had three more months together before that became their reality.

Lina had just closed the fridge door behind her when Juan sauntered into the room. She nearly dropped the food container, which made him smirk.

Wow.

He looked... irresistible.

His outfit wasn't at all what she'd expected him to choose. He was dressed in black from head to toe, the fabric molded to his muscled body like it was painted on.

"You..." Words! Where were all the words? She moved her hand up and down. "You look..."

"Yes?" Juan quirked his brows, his eyes twinkling with mischief.

"You surprised me, that's all." She fumbled with the lid of the container.

Juan laughed and came up behind her. Brushing her hair to the side, he kissed her neck, setting off butterflies in her stomach and sending goosebumps across her skin.

"I didn't know you owned clothes that are just one color," she quipped, feeling his smile against her skin.

"I figured I might as well complement your outfit while also wearing something that doesn't attract that much attention."

"Yeah, well, that might've worked if you hadn't chosen something that highlights every contour of your action figure physique."

His laughter vibrated against her shoulder.

The black slacks and button-down shirt he wore matched her outfit. She was sporting black and white striped high-waisted pants, belted and paired with a black cap-sleeved shirt.

Juan turned her around to face him.

How weird was it that after two months of being in his orbit, her heart still fluttered when she stood so close to him?

His thumb traced her bottom lip and because she was feeling bold, she bit his finger and then swirled her tongue around it to ease the sting.

His gaze darkened and he stroked his palm down her throat, over the curve of her breast, and down to her waist.

Gripping her hips, Juan hoisted her up onto the kitchen island, moving her thighs apart and stepping between them. Lina's breath released on a gasp when his erection pressed into her.

"I like how you look in those pants," he said, his voice husky, "but they are impractical. I have zero access to the good parts." He rocked his pelvis into hers once more before he gave her a firm kiss and stepped away.

She fanned herself and clenched her thighs. "To be fair, when I bought these clothes it never occurred to me that one day I'd have a man who wants access to the goods all the time."

He braced himself against the opposite counter and let out an audible breath. "You're so not helping." He gestured at the bulge in his pants. "I'm trying to think of something unsexy so we can leave the house."

But why waste a perfectly good erection?

Lina hopped off the counter and trailed her fingers over the front of his pants.

He grasped her wrist but she shook him off. "Lina," he said when she pulled down the zipper.

She had his pants open in no time and palmed his length over his briefs, keeping her gaze locked on his. When she wetted her lips with the tip of her tongue his gaze flicked down to her mouth.

As she slid her hand under the fabric and stroked his silky skin, Juan pushed two fingers past her lips so she could show him what was yet to come.

When Lina sped up her movements, his eyes drifted shut.

"Look at me," she said and his eyes opened. Holding his gaze, she went down on her knees.

His fingers curled in her hair, tight enough to tingle but not hard enough to hurt. That was his superpower—he expertly skirted the line between pleasure and pain, inching her out of her comfort zone just enough to make it exciting.

Lina pushed down his pants a little more to give her access to his phenomenal butt. He groaned when she pressed her fingers into his firm cheek while stroking him with her other hand, her tongue swirling around the crown of his jutting erection.

When he moaned, she took him in as deep as she could go, eliciting a curse from him. Losing all restraint, he thrust in short bursts, and Lina held on to his thigh so she didn't lose her footing.

Juan came fast and hard and she felt drunk with power.

"You're a queen," he said hoarsely as he helped her up and kissed her deeply.

***

By the time they pulled up in front of the gallery, it was later than intended. Juan helped her out of the car and paid the valet. They had barely taken five steps toward the entrance before someone shouted his name. Not his actual name, but Manolo, the moniker attached to his fame.

When Lina tensed, Juan gave her hand a squeeze, then waved to the fan before he guided her into the building.

Inside, it only got worse. Eyes trailed their every move, and a couple of people whispered and giggled. Lina's skin crawled with all the attention, making her want to turn around and go home.

How were they supposed to admire the art installation when they had unwillingly become the main attraction?

Juan made an effort to keep his features and their conversation pleasant but the tick in his jaw was a dead giveaway that he wasn't enjoying himself either.

When they stopped in front of a wooden sculpture whose twisted form could be interpreted as either a flower or the folds of a vulva, Lina leaned closer to Juan and whispered, "I don't know how to act. This is not my idea of fun."

He turned to face her, his lips pressed tight. "I know this is uncomfortable, but this isn't going away anytime soon. I'm a public figure and that attracts attention whether I want it or not. Ask your dad or your brother, it's the same for them."

She remembered how everyone had reacted when Manuel crossed the restaurant the first time they met. Would people be taking pictures of them this time too?

"You have two choices," Juan said, tucking his arm around her waist. "We can let them ruin our evening, or you can give me your full attention and pretend they aren't there."

She had no answer, so he turned back toward the sculpture and cocked his head. "Bears a strong resemblance to your pretty vagina."

A laugh burst free from her chest, making the decision for her. "Should we get this for our bedroom?"

This time, Juan's smile was genuine and heart-stopping. As he began to entertain her with his outrageous theories about the sculpture, Lina looped her arm around his waist, grateful to share another blissful moment with him.

CHAPTER 13

*Love triangles & a blast
from the past*

The next day, Lina was in the middle of painting a piece for an up-and-coming Colombian jewelry designer when her phone rang on the coffee table.

Juan was lounging on the couch with Ervin while she worked at the dining table. "It's your brother," he announced.

"Can you pick it up?"

"Yo. Lina's working so I'm putting you on speaker."

Her brother's voice filled the room. "How was your evening? Enjoy any shows?"

Lina's hand stilled.

"Let me guess," Juan sat up and reached for the phone, "someone took a picture."

"Oh man," her brother chuckled, "It's better. Hang on, I'll send it to you."

Abandoning her work, Lina joined Juan on the sofa. He'd just opened the link and started reading the headline. *"Surprise Sighting: Manuel Campos's*

Mystery Girlfriend Causes Stir by Attending Art Show with Rival Singer Manolo!" Juan covered the screen with his hand when Lina tried to read the article.

"Hey, I was reading that."

"Nope. It's not a flattering story. For either of us." He put the phone back on the coffee table.

"How do you want to address this?" her brother asked.

"How about we don't, and you and John update your Wikipedia entries instead?" Juan's tone was harder than she'd ever heard it.

When she raised her brows at him, he said, "That's at the root of it, Lina. If Manuel claimed you as his sister and John as his daughter—the way it should be—I wouldn't look like an ass for stealing someone else's girl, and it would be obvious how I'm connected to you since I was in the same movie as your dad."

"I'm not going to ask that of them." She put her hand on Juan's fist. "This is going to affect my dad's family and Manu's family."

Juan massaged the space between his eyes with his free hand. "Why is it that you always have to suffer for other people's choices?"

She opened her mouth, but he shook his head. "They're *grown-ups*, and they need to take responsibility for their actions."

"He's right, Lina," her brother agreed. "The damage has already been done. Now it's up to our families how they want to move forward. Even if acknowledging your existence breaks both our parents' marriages, they are responsible, not you."

Lina pressed the heels of her hands to her temples and closed her eyes, only to lose her orientation because Juan pulled her on top of him and locked her in a bear hug.

"You still there?" Manuel asked with a sigh when no one spoke for a while.

"Yeah." Juan tightened his hold on her for a second. "She just needs a moment."

"I'm sorry," her brother muttered, his voice raspy. "I'm going to give her dad a call to make sure Lina gets added to his entry too. This needs to happen now. The secrecy isn't fair to either of you."

The line went dead, and Lina burrowed her face against Juan's chest. His heartbeat started slowing down, calming hers in the process. She couldn't remember how long they stayed that way. They must have fallen asleep at some point because when Lina opened her eyes the moon shone through the floor-to-ceiling windows.

Juan brushed the hair away from her face, a gesture so tender she hugged him tighter. "You okay?" He played with her hair, and she relished the way it felt against her scalp.

"No," she said, bunching the fabric of his shirt in her fist.

"It's okay to be not okay," he sang the Imagine Dragons song to her, making her chuckle.

"Do you think we're going to get married one day?" she asked, apparently out loud because his hand stilled for a moment before he continued stroking her.

"Yeah, why?"

"You're awesome. I want to keep you forever."

"I'm with you, married or not."

"Promise?"

He held out his pinkie finger to her and she hooked hers around his.

***

Two hours later, they were cozied up in Juan's theater room, sharing popcorn and nachos. Juan's phone chimed, and he picked it up, showing Lina the text message he received. It instructed him to turn on a specific TV channel.

Juan paused the movie and switched to the requested channel, revealing an entertainment news program.

Lina's heartbeat sped up when her brother's face appeared on the screen. He was connected via video chat, sporting white earbuds.

The interview began with the news anchor congratulating Manuel on his new single debuting at number one. Lina felt a swell of pride, although she doubted it was the reason he'd sent Juan that message.

Then they brought up the controversy surrounding Manuel's alleged new relationship, and it clicked.

He smiled knowingly. "It never ceases to amaze me what bullshit the tabloids come up with."

The young newscaster pretended to be shocked.

"So you're not involved in a love triangle with Manolo and the mystery woman who's been seen with both of you?"

"The only thing they got right was the chemistry between Manolo and his girlfriend."

Lina's gaze snapped to Juan, who was smiling at the TV.

"People of the Internet," her brother teased, "Get this: my alleged rival is dating my sister! She's awesome, and so is he, so let them be. That's all I'm going to say on the subject."

Lina turned to Juan, her voice filled with uncertainty. "You're okay with this?"

"That everyone knows I'm off the market?" he replied with a grin.

She nodded. "You're about to go on tour. Doesn't that kill the fantasy?"

Juan's expression softened. "The number of fucks I give about that is zero. I'm not willing to sacrifice our happiness just to please my record label." He gestured towards the TV, his words biting with sarcasm. "Are *you* okay with this? I know I'm every parent's dream choice for a future son-in-law."

"You should be," she said in response to his self-depreciation. If people couldn't see past his looks and the image he projected on stage, they were missing out. "I've never been treated better. No one makes me laugh and smile the way you do. No one makes me come harder."

He laughed at her candidness.

"I'm serious, Juan. I love being your girlfriend. If

you're okay with it, I'm okay with it."

***

Juan had to go out of town for a couple of days, so Lina made the decision to bring Ervin to her place until he returned, even though Juan had assured her she was welcome to stay at his house.

His place was awesome, but she missed her own. They'd been honest about their attachment to their respective homes as both of them saw their estates as symbols of their journey from poverty to hard-earned success. So they agreed to keep both properties even when they lived together.

As strong as the temptation was to immerse herself in her next project, Lina decided to take a break, reflecting on everything that had happened over the past two months. Meeting Juan, painting and completing her best work yet, her dad being back in her life, the new brother she suddenly had...

Just as she was lost in her thoughts, her dad's name appeared on her phone, making her heart race. For a moment, she considered letting it go to voicemail, but she wanted to reconnect with him, and answering the phone was the first step.

"Hello?"

"Lina, this is Samantha."

Nausea tightened her gut, her mind screaming at her to hang up the phone.

"Your dad would never allow me to call you, so please don't be mad at him." Samantha's voice was tinged with apprehension.

Lina struggled to speak, and after a few moments of silence, her stepmother continued. "I'm so glad you and your dad have reconciled."

"But?" Lina pressed, bracing herself for what would come next.

"No 'but.' I understand that we've never had the mother-daughter relationship we both deserved. I was young and completely unprepared when you came into my life. I know there are things I should have done differently."

"I don't think it would have made a difference, Sam." Lina sighed, taking ownership of her own actions as an adult. "The same outcome would've likely occurred with any other woman. My dad was my whole world, and I didn't want anyone to come between us. In my young mind, I couldn't comprehend that he could love both of us or that *you* could love me."

Samantha sniffled on the other end of the line, and Lina blinked back tears.

Settling into an armchair facing the window with a mesmerizing view of nature beyond it, Lina admitted, "It was a simple belief I held onto. Since my mother didn't want me, I couldn't fathom that any other woman would want me either. It's a distorted way of thinking that I still struggle with, despite knowing better."

"Does that mean we'll never have a close relationship?"

"It means I need therapy." She had to work through her own deep-seated issues, no way around it.

They lapsed into silence, each lost in their own thoughts until Samantha spoke again. "Valeria and Luca would like to get to know you."

Lina's other half-siblings likely had no memory of her because of their young age when she left.

"Your dad showed them the mural you painted for Manolo. Valeria is a huge fan of your boyfriend, so you instantly became the coolest person ever. I must confess though, I made her take down the poster of his naked, tattooed body. Your dad nearly had an aneurysm when he walked into her room two years ago."

They both shared a small laugh.

"I can only imagine his reaction when he found out his eldest daughter is dating him," Samantha remarked, a chuckle in her voice. "I wish I could've been there to witness it."

"He took it well, considering he was more concerned about me accidentally dating my *brother*."

"Who happens to be your sister's other favorite singer. I made her take down his poster too. Less controversy and tattoos, but still too much naked skin."

Lina pressed a fist against her lips. "Sex sells, unfortunately. But as someone who benefits from those muscles, I can't complain or I'd be a hypocrite."

"Tell me about it. Your dad's biceps still make me weak in the knees."

Lina cringed, but couldn't help but smile. "Ew, Sam. That's more than I ever wanted to know about my dad's sex life."

Changing the subject, Samantha said, "I was hoping you would come visit us soon. We'd love to have you."

When Lina remained silent, Samantha added, "Juan is welcome too. Your dad said he makes you feel safe."

"I'll think about it." If she stayed in L.A. while Juan was on his world tour, she wouldn't feel as lonely. "Can I bring my dog?"

Warmth filtered into Samantha's words. "Of course."

CHAPTER 14

So it goes…

Lina spent the rest of the day indulging in self-care. She journaled, meditated, bathed, and applied various moisturizing masks from her collection, which helped restore her inner calm. Ervin, her faithful companion, slept on the couch, undisturbed by her activities.

As the evening approached, the sound of the doorbell interrupted the tranquility.

Lina hesitated as she glanced at the camera feed.

Who is that?

The unfamiliar car made her pretend she wasn't home.

The doorbell rang again a minute later. All the relaxation she had achieved over the past few hours went out the window.

Lina checked the camera again, this time noticing a woman stepping out of the car. She appeared to be around Samantha's age, with blond hair and dressed in a sophisticated champagne-colored pantsuit.

Though her complexion leaned towards the lighter side, her facial features reflected her Colombian heritage.

Summoning her courage, Lina spoke into the speaker, "Hello?"

"Angelina, I am Marisol Valencia, Manuel's mother. I would like to speak with you," came the voice from the other side of the iron gate.

Manuel's mother. Right. A surge of anger propelled Lina off the sofa and towards the stranger who had given birth to her.

With each step down the driveway, she felt a mix of anticipation and dread, unsure of what to expect from this long-awaited encounter.

As Lina approached, a chill ran through her despite the warm evening air. She didn't know what she expected from facing her birth mother, but it wasn't this. Before she could utter a single word, Marisol's harsh bark reverberated through the air, filled with resentment and hostility.

"I hope you're proud of yourself, you little bitch. You destroyed my marriage and turned my son against me! I should have aborted you when I had the chance. Your whole existence is a mistake."

Lina's heart thumped wildly as Marisol's words struck like physical blows, slicing away at her carefully constructed armor.

"Just look at who you chose to be with, that man disgusts me! No daughter of mine would have picked such a vile man." Marisol turned towards her car, pausing only to deliver a final warning. "Stay away from my son. And *please*, crawl back into that hole you were hiding in. We're all better off that way."

Lina stood frozen, her gaze fixed on the retreating vehicle. The impact of the woman's disdain was so overwhelming, her broken pieces spilled out onto the cobblestone driveway. She kept heaving long after her stomach contents formed a puddle at her feet.

Stunned and trembling, Lina struggled to regain her composure, her lungs burning and her belly constricting.

Summoning her last reserves of strength, she managed to make her way back to her house, barely able to support herself. She collapsed in the hallway and curled up into a ball.

Sensing her distress, Ervin circled around her with gentle nudges and paw taps, his cries mirroring her anguish.

Dizzy and drained, Lina found solace in the warmth of the puppy's body as he lay down beside her, his head resting on her arm.

***

Juan felt his sanity slipping away. Why wasn't Lina answering her phone? It had only been two days since he left, but her silence made him question everything.

Could those two days be enough to change her mind about their relationship?

Don't be stupid, man, he chided himself, trying to shake off the doubt. She'd asked him about their future together, about marriage. That meant she was committed.

But still, the absence of her response gnawed at him. He'd called her yesterday afternoon, hoping for a sign that she was alright. Now, it was already two o'clock the following day, and he hadn't heard a word from her.

The unease grew the longer his texts went unanswered. Driving to her house to check on her was what he wanted to do, but he couldn't. He was in Miami recording a collaboration and generating anticipation for his upcoming tour.

All he knew for certain was that Lina wasn't at his place, as he'd checked the security cameras.

Feeling desperate, he decided to dial both her dad and her brother. Thankfully, they both accepted the conference video call.

"Has either of you heard from Lina?" Juan asked, unable to conceal the urgency in his voice.

"No, why?" John's tone mirrored his concern. Manuel too seemed suspicious. They likely wondered if he'd done something to upset Lina, like cheating on her or displaying his alleged machismo.

Juan swallowed his aggravation. "I can't reach her. And no, we didn't have a fight or anything that would make her shut me out. I have this feeling that something's wrong, but I'm too far away to swing by her house."

"I'm on my way. I'll call once I get there," Manuel declared before ending the call.

"I swear I didn't do anything," Juan told John as he

rubbed his eyes. "I'm really fucking scared."

"I believe you, son," John reassured him, his voice steady and comforting. "It's going to be okay."

Thirty minutes later, Manuel initiated another conference call. "I'm here, but she doesn't answer. I don't know the code to open the gate... Juan, I think you're right, something feels wrong. There's a puddle of dried-up vomit here."

Every nerve in Juan's body fired at once, leaving him shaky and nauseated. He quickly shared the gate and house codes with Manuel, urging him to hurry.

Manuel hopped into his car, leaving the phone on the passenger seat as he drove to Lina's house.

At the entrance door, they heard the sharp intake of Manuel's breath. "It's not locked."

Then the line went dead, leaving Juan and John in a state of panic.

"John," Juan choked, his voice trembling as he fought back tears.

"We have to wait and pray," John said, his words heavy.

They remained on the call but didn't speak. The silence stretched on, each moment feeling like an eternity.

An hour later, Manuel's request to rejoin their video call broke the deafening silence, and Juan's pulse quickened in his ears.

Manuel's worn-out and disheveled appearance was enough to confirm that something wasn't right.

"Sorry I dropped the call," Manuel said, his

shoulders slumping. "It was for your own good. And before I say anything else, focus on the fact that she's going to be okay."

The words hit Juan like a punch to the gut. She wasn't okay now. Overwhelmed with emotions, he dropped his face into his hands. Fear mingled with relief as he held onto Manuel's reassurance that Lina would be alright.

"I can't tell you exactly what happened because Lina isn't responsive." Manuel's voice broadcasted his frustration. "But the doctor informed me that she's severely dehydrated, and her cortisol and AChE levels were abnormally high."

John's brows furrowed. "What does that mean?"

Manuel tensed ever so slightly. "It could indicate that she experienced something stressful or terrifying." Whether it was due to a single event or the accumulation of everything she'd been through in the past week was hard to say without being able to speak with her.

Manuel paused for a moment. "The police were also involved. They want to review the security footage. It's strange that the door was open. I found her near the entrance, and if the vomit by the gate was hers, it seems like she hardly made it inside."

John's eyes widened. "The vomit was on her side of the gate?"

Manuel nodded. "But until we can talk to her or review the footage, it's all speculation." Probably sensing the need for a shift in conversation, he said, "On a slightly brighter note, I thought it might bring you some comfort that your puppy has been watching over her. I couldn't bring him into the hospital, so he's waiting in the car."

As much as he loved his dog, Juan knew he had to give Ervin to Lina—the two of them had a special connection, and he wanted her to have someone who would always love her unconditionally.

"I'm going to fly back as soon as I can get a hold of the pilot," Juan assured them.

"I'll see if I can take Lin-Miguel's jet," John said, mirroring his urgency. "Keep us posted in the meantime."

They ended the call, and Juan forced himself to get up and start packing. Every movement felt like a struggle, his body weighed down by worry and fear. But he pushed through, refusing to let his discomfort deter him.

With each item he placed in his suitcase, he mentally prepared himself for what lay ahead.

CHAPTER 15

I got you, babe

When Juan arrived at the hospital in the early morning hours, he found Manuel pacing in front of a closed door. They fell into a hug.

"Any news?" Juan asked, his stomach rolling.

Manuel huffed out a frustrated sigh. "She's awake, but she's not talking. She hasn't spoken a word to the doctor, the police, or even me."

Realization dawned on Juan as he chewed his lip. "She gets like that whenever her abandonment issues are triggered. Before we got together, she once avoided me for two days before I figured out she was doing it because she got spooked."

He hoped it wasn't him leaving for Miami that had caused her to lock herself up inside her head. "What she really needs is a therapist—she's mentioned that a lot lately." He placed a comforting hand on Manuel's shoulder. "Thank you for being there for her. She's lucky to have you as her brother."

Manuel leaned against the wall, his hands

trembling with fatigue.

"You need to go home and get some rest. We'll talk later, and I promise to keep you updated."

Manuel hesitated for a moment, but then nodded and gave Juan a bro hug before making his way home.

Until John arrived, Juan had to navigate the hospital on his own. Fortunately, being Manolo had its perks, and in this particular instance, he vowed to shamelessly use his fame to his advantage.

A smile for a picture was all it took to open doors and gain cooperation from the hospital staff.

Juan's breath caught in his throat when the nurse led him into Lina's room. The suite was as spacious and bright as he'd expected, a reflection of her brother's thoughtfulness.

Lina was sitting up, her gaze fixed on the window. She didn't respond when the nurse called her name.

"Lina," Juan tried, keeping his voice tender. Though she didn't turn to face him, he sensed a flicker of recognition in her body.

"Can you give us a moment?" he asked the nurse, who obliged and left, closing the door behind her.

Uncertain of what to do, Juan sat on the edge of the bed and took Lina's limp hand in his. She closed her eyes, shutting down any possibility of conversation before it even began.

Despite the weight of her silence, he leaned back against the pillows, drawing her close to his chest. She didn't embrace him as she normally would, but she instinctively inhaled his scent. That was the one power he knew he held: Lina loved the scent of him.

Juan began stroking her, and after some time, her hand clenched onto his shirt—another small win.

An hour or so later, a knock echoed through the room.

John came inside, releasing a deep breath as he sank into the chair beside the bed.

"She doesn't want to talk," Juan said, careful not to wake Lina.

"About what happened?"

Juan shook his head. "She hasn't uttered a single word since she regained consciousness."

John's eyes reflected a mix of sadness and understanding. "I remember her doing that as a child. It used to happen when... when..."

"When something triggered her abandonment issues?" Juan finished John's sentence.

"Yes. It was her response to feeling rejected or unworthy," John recalled, rubbing his eyes wearily. "Did they find anything on the security tapes?"

"I don't know. I don't have access to that information. It's a miracle they even let me in here."

In the eyes of the law, he was no one to her. His resentment of that fact must have been obvious, because John asked, "You're going to marry her after this?"

"I was planning on marrying her regardless, so why wait?"

John nodded, biting his bottom lip. "Let me see what I can find out." He pressed a kiss to Lina's head before heading out.

Left alone with Lina, Juan draped his arms around her, holding her close. She stirred but remained asleep, so he closed his eyes too.

Their peaceful moment ended when a doctor came into the room to examine her.

Juan loosened his hold on her, but Lina still clung to him, unwilling to let go completely. "Can you work around me?"

The doctor offered a sympathetic smile. "It might be a little awkward, but I'll do my best."

Despite the added challenge, the doctor continued with the examination.

Eventually, she gave them the reassuring news that Lina could go home as long as she drank plenty of electrolytes and rested. The doctor attributed her lack of speech and avoidance of eye contact to psychological factors, recommending that she see a psychiatrist for treatment.

During the drive home, Lina remained silent, her gaze trained on the passing scenery.
Juan knew she felt safe at his place, so he took her there, hoping some comfort and familiarity would help her recover.

***

Once inside the house, Lina retreated to the couch while Juan anxiously awaited John's arrival, hoping her dad had uncovered something helpful.

When John finally arrived, his appearance mirrored the weariness and anguish that Manuel had displayed earlier. His complexion was pale, and his eyes held a haunted expression.

Juan felt as if his legs might give way beneath him. "I take it you found something?"

John nodded. "I saw the footage. Marisol confronted her. Imagine the worst thing someone could say to you. That's how horrifying it was."

"Marisol?"

"Manuel's mother."

"I want to see it."

"Don't. It'll haunt your dreams. Some things can't be unseen or unheard."

Juan slumped against the wall, his exhaustion overtaking him.

"Lina needs professional help to get through this," John continued. "It's astounding to me how such a spiteful woman could bring two incredibly loving and selfless people into this world. If Manuel ever discovers what his mother did, it will shatter him."

The gravity of the situation sank in, leaving Juan feeling drained and defeated.

"We're going to find her the best psychiatrist in the city," John promised. "I'll stay here until she gets better. We're family, and we'll face this together."

John guided Juan upstairs and covered him with a throw blanket, offering a comforting gesture that made Juan feel five years old.

"I'll bring Lina up here. Even if she can't express her feelings right now, she wants to be near you. The doctor mentioned how she clung to you earlier."

Juan fought against his heavy eyelids, determined to stay awake until Lina was settled beside him.

Once she joined him, he cradled her in his arms, holding her tightly and inhaling her scent. "I don't know if you can hear me in the state you're in, but I want you to know how much I love you. We have an incredible future ahead of us once you recover. We don't let the bullies win."

Lina didn't respond, but a tear escaped, tracing its path onto his arm, telling him she heard him just fine.

***

When Juan woke up the next morning, Lina was still sleeping, her body pressed against his. He longed to kiss her awake and hear the sound of her voice, but he resisted, not wanting to disturb her rest.

Quietly slipping out of bed, he made his way downstairs to the living room where he found John dozing on the sofa.

"Why didn't you take one of the guest rooms?"

"I did, but I couldn't sleep anymore. How did the night go?"

"She didn't wake up." He pressed his palm to his forehead, wincing. "I ache all over. I can only imagine how Lina must be feeling."

John nodded. "Sleep is the best thing for her right now. We just need to ensure she stays hydrated."

Juan felt a wave of uncertainty wash over him. How would they convince Lina to drink enough fluids if she refused? Before he could voice his concerns, John preempted his thoughts.

"Since I can't sleep, I researched the best

psychiatrists in town. I have a shortlist of three."

"It's so hard not being able to talk to her." Or kiss her, Juan confessed, the frustration and longing pushing him closer to the breaking point. "Part of me wants to shake her, or do something to provoke a reaction."

"Patience is a virtue for a reason," John said with a faint smile. "I understand your feelings though. It took me a long time and lots of practice to master the skill."

Juan slumped onto the couch beside John, placing his phone on the coffee table.

Almost immediately, the screen lit up with a message from Manuel.

John's expression turned grave. "We might have a bit of a problem," he said, gesturing toward the phone.

Juan's heart sank. "Why?"

"He wants to see her, but I'm concerned that she won't want that," John explained. "Marisol threatened her to stay away from him, or else."

Juan cursed under his breath. "And you think she might give him up... Maybe we need a family therapist too. There are too many variables and people involved."

"I'm on it," John assured him, rising from the couch. "I'll have someone here by the end of the day."

Juan sent a text to Manuel, updating him on Lina's condition and asking if he could watch Ervin until they had a chance to speak with a psychiatrist.

Then he grabbed a sports drink from the fridge

and headed back upstairs to check on Lina.

CHAPTER 16

*Follow your heart (or
your magic stick)*

When Juan entered the room, he found Lina still curled up on the bed, her gaze resting on the peaceful nature outside the window.

He placed the bottle on the nightstand and spoke, his voice gentle yet firm, "I know you don't want to talk, but you can hear me. It's important that you drink this, so please don't fight me on this."

Lina didn't make eye contact, but she reached out and grabbed the bottle, drinking about half of it before returning it to the nightstand.

"If you know anything about me, you know I'm not a patient, passive man," he grumbled as he took a seat next to her. "I had every intention of leaving you be until you were ready. But I'm also your partner, and I'm here. And maybe that counts for something."

Juan placed a hand on her cheek and tilted her face towards him. "I understand why you put up these walls. What you've been through is despicable, and I'm not going to minimize that. But you're strong, and you're a fighter. That woman who brought you into the world—*she* is messed up in the head. Deep down, you know she said those things because she is hurting and desperate, not because they are true."

He touched his forehead to Lina's, their connection grounding him. "You're such a gift. Everyone who's ever had the privilege to get to know you feels that way. I promise to keep reminding you of how awesome you are. You are loved, and you are not alone in this."

Juan remained close as they both sat in the quiet room. He knew it would take time and patience, but he was determined to help her rebuild the strength within her.

He held his breath when the magic happened. Lina brushed her lips against his, and before she could retreat, he cupped her neck and deepened the kiss, his heart hammering in his chest.

As he gripped her hips and pulled her closer, she brought her legs around him and clenched her hand on his back. A freeing groan ripped from his chest when she started moving against him.

He kissed her like the gift she was, pressing her into the mattress. They both pulled their sweats and underwear down enough so he could slide inside her, her moans the wordless language that affirmed her feelings for him.

Lina fastened him to her, the tight hold restricting their movements but maximizing friction. There was nothing better than to be this close to her, to feel how much she wanted him, and to show her how much he craved her in return.

She scraped her teeth against his clavicle as she came, and he followed when her muscles contracted around him.

They stayed locked together for a long time.

Juan's hand remained under the back of Lina's shirt as he gently stroked her. Lina reciprocated, her hand tracing soothing patterns on his back. The warmth of their bodies pressed together created an unexpected sense of security and stability amidst the chaos that had unfolded in their lives.

When the doorbell rang an hour later, they moved apart.

Juan handed her a tissue but first, he trailed his finger between her folds and spread his cum. It was the first time they had sex without a condom. Lina had an IUD and they'd agreed to risk it after they'd gotten tested.

Juan placed a kiss on her clit before he gave her space to clean up.

Once their clothes were in place, he held out a hand for her and pulled her to her feet. They kept holding hands as they headed downstairs and into the foyer.

"Dad," was the first word that left Lina's lips.

John's face transformed from sorrow to elation as he stepped forward and gave Lina a bear hug. "My baby," he cried.

Juan watched them for a moment before his gaze

flicked to the other person in the room—an elderly woman who smiled warmly as they witnessed the father-daughter moment.

"You must be Juan," she said, holding her hand out to him.

John created some space between himself and Lina to introduce them. "Sweetheart, this is Marta Bahamón. I asked her to help us work through what happened."

"Us?" Lina asked, her gaze flitting between Juan and her dad.

Juan took the opportunity to respond since it was his idea. "We're in this together. I clearly have a lot to learn because I did the opposite of what I was supposed to do to help you through this."

John smiled. "Hey, you went with your gut and it worked."

Lina tapped her lips. "Hm... Was it really your gut?"

Juan pinched her side, making her squeal. "What can I say, I got the magic stick."

Lina gaped, but her eyes twinkled. "I can't believe you said that."

He shot her a look that said, *really?*

"I can't believe you said that in front of my dad and this lovely woman," Lina amended, gesturing at them.

Nothing made him happier than seeing her come back to life.

Juan lifted his hands. "It might be important for our therapist to know that physical touch is my love language."

Lina's gaze went soft as she placed her palm over his heart. With a smile, she pressed up on her toes and gave him a tender kiss.

Fanning himself, he pretended to be scandalized. "I can't believe you did that—in front of your dad and this lovely woman."

"What?" She wrapped her arms around his waist. "Physical touch is my love language too."

Marta Bahamón leaned closer to John. "They have a solid foundation, that's a promising start."

Juan gestured for them to have a seat in the living room as the doorbell chimed again. He knew who was at the door, and hopefully, he'd made the right call there too.

Manuel came inside, holding onto Ervin who started barking with excitement upon seeing them. He released the energetic puppy with a tired but affectionate smile, and the dog happily bounced between Lina and Juan.

Lina embraced the dog and nuzzled her face against his fur.

The therapist, observing the interaction, expressed her approval. "This is good for her too." Then, turning her attention to Manuel, she asked, "And who are you, young man?"

At that moment, Lina finally turned toward her brother.

Manuel's voice broke. "I'm so sorry for what my mother did to you. I didn't... I didn't think she..."

Juan squeezed his shoulder, a silent show of support that helped Manuel find his voice.

"You're my sister, Lina, and I want you in my life. Please don't let someone else's misguided actions get between us."

Lina stood, her hands trembling. "I want you in my life too. But she threatened me, and I'm terrified of what she might do if she ever finds out. I mean, how did she even know where I live?"

Manuel wrung his hands. "That's the strange thing: she's been keeping tabs on you since you were little."

John's eyebrows furrowed in confusion. "How do you know?"

Juan guided them into the living room.

Manuel took a deep breath before explaining, "After I confronted her, I saw her pull out a box from her closet. One of those keepsake boxes with flowers on it. She looked at the contents for a moment, and even though I couldn't see her face, I could tell she was crying. When she left the room, I sneaked in there and found the box. It was hidden behind another keepsake box filled with things from my life."

He rubbed his temple. "The box she'd been looking at contained documents and photos. Your birth certificate, yearbook, graduation pictures, even a picture of your dad. I didn't have much time to go through everything, but those were a few things I saw."

As Lina slumped forward, burying her face in her hands, Juan stroked her back.

The therapist told them, "Giving away a child is a

profoundly traumatic experience, regardless of how one tries to rationalize it. Part of her couldn't truly let go, and she may have fantasized about what could have been if she had made a different choice."

Turning to face Lina, the therapist said, "I reviewed the footage from the security cameras. It seems that she appeared as two different personas —the one forced to confront the consequences of her actions and choosing to blame you, and the 'fantasy mother' who disapproved of your choice in a partner."

Juan fought to control his anger, but the therapist noticed his clenched fist. Lina did too and wrapped her hand around it.

Lina's voice, gentle but determined, broke through the building tension. "Look at me," she said, and he turned to meet her gaze. "I see you for who you are, and I know how fortunate I am to have you in my life. Anyone who disagrees can go to hell."

Juan couldn't help but let a smirk escape his lips. "Consider this your fair warning," he playfully declared, addressing everyone in the room.

With a swift motion, he slid his fingers into Lina's hair and affirmed his promise to her with a resolute kiss.

ABOUT THE AUTHOR

As both an immigrant and a bit of a free spirit herself, Alex writes romance novels that challenge the status quo. Her love of music, cultures, personal development, and the many unconventional people she has met along the way, inspired her family saga *Rebels Like Us*.

After spending most of her life in Germany, Italy, Ireland, Colombia, and California, she currently lives in the foothills of the Wasatch Mountains with her two favorite guys.

www.alexbenkast.com